I STILL Love YOU

Nine Things Troubled Kids Need from Their Parents

Michael Ungar
Ph.D.

DUNDURN
TORONTO

I STILL

Love

YOU

CALGARY PUBLIC LIBRARY

MAR   2015

Copyright © Michael Ungar, 2015

All rights reserved. No part of this publication may be reproduced, stored in a retrieval system, or transmitted in any form or by any means, electronic, mechanical, photo-copying, recording, or otherwise (except for brief passages for purposes of review) without the prior permission of Dundurn Press. Permission to photocopy should be requested from Access Copyright.

The cue cards starting on page 203 may be photocopied for personal use, but no other part of the book may be reproduced without permission from the publisher.

Project editor: Carrie Gleason
Copy-editor: Natalie Meditsky
Design: Colleen Wormald
Cover Design: Laura Boyle
Cover Image: ©iStockphoto/jc_design
Printer: Webcom

Library and Archives Canada Cataloguing in Publication

Ungar, Michael, 1963-, author
    I still love you : nine things troubled kids need from their parents / Michael Ungar.

Issued in print and electronic formats.
ISBN 978-1-4597-2983-4 (pbk.).--ISBN 978-1-4597-2984-1 (pdf).--
ISBN 978-1-4597-2985-8 (epub)

    1. Parenting. 2. Problem children--Behavior modification.
3. Behavior disorders in children--Treatment. I. Title.

HQ755.8.U65 2014   649'.1   C2014-904994-3
                                          C2014-904995-1

1   2   3   4   5   19   18   17   16   15

We acknowledge the support of the Canada Council for the Arts and the Ontario Arts Council for our publishing program. We also acknowledge the financial support of the Government of Canada through the Canada Book Fund and Livres Canada Books, and the Government of Ontario through the Ontario Book Publishing Tax Credit and the Ontario Media Development Corporation.

Care has been taken to trace the ownership of copyright material used in this book. The author and the publisher welcome any information enabling them to rectify any references or credits in subsequent editions.
                                                          J. Kirk Howard, President

The publisher is not responsible for websites or their content unless they are owned by the publisher.

Printed and bound in Canada.

Visit us at
Dundurn.com | @dundurnpress | Facebook.com/dundurnpress | Pinterest.com/dundurnpress

Dundurn
3 Church Street, Suite 500
Toronto, Ontario, Canada
M5E 1M2

"We are all better when we're loved."
— Alistair MacLeod, *No Great Mischief*

Contents

Disclaimer

The Children and Their Families

In order to protect the privacy of all the individuals with whom I have had the privilege of working, the reader must know that the stories I share in these pages are simultaneously real and imagined. Though they are based on the lived experience of the many young people and their families I have met through my research and clinical practice, I have changed their stories to preserve their confidentiality. Only my own story is true and then only to the limits of my memory and whatever poetic licence I have taken to make sense of my experience as a child. Though none of the families portrayed actually exist as I describe them, some readers might think they recognize in these pages someone in particular. I would suggest the resemblance is more coincidental than factual.

In contrast, the research reported in this book is true and complete to the best of my knowledge. However, this book is intended only as an informative guide for those wishing to know more about parenting issues. In no way is this book intended to replace, countermand, or conflict with the advice given to you by your own health-care provider. The ultimate decision concerning care should be made between you and a professional. I strongly recommend you follow his or her advice if you find it sound. My publisher and I must, of course, disclaim all liability in connection with the use of this book.

No More Problem Children

We know what to do to prevent children from tumbling into lives of chaos and pain. If you have a problem child, or are worried your child is becoming one, trust me, change can happen.

I know because I should have become one of those problem children with labels like "delinquent," "disordered," "addicted," "anxious," and "truant." My children might argue I fit those labels some days, but they don't mean it. The cycle has been broken. They are great kids, as wonderful as the hundreds of children and adolescents who have come to see me and shed their troubled selves.

That, of course, is not what they're like when we first meet in my office with their families, in juvenile detention centres, on the street, in the hospital, or in the shelters and foster homes where they are supposed to be staying. Meeting them for the first time, I think, "My life could have been just as full of problems." They walk with difficulty, as if they're wearing heavy woollen coats in a wet November snowstorm. Even when they swagger and purposely bully those around them, or try to hide, threaten suicide, or refuse to go to school, you can see the effort they're making to hold their fragile lives together.

If you listen closely to the silly, hurtful things they yell at the adults in their lives, you'll hear the strain in their voices as they plead for someone to convince them they're special, untarnished, and loved. I know that voice and how it feels to be abandoned. I also know what it means to shed my heavy winter coat and stand shivering in the cold, looking for someone to help me make something of myself.

My life now hides my troubled start. I sit at a desk in a bright, sunny corner office at a prestigious research university. I should be in some darker place. I should be angry and alone. I'm not. My children should hate me. They don't. I've spent two decades wondering why I was able to shake the legacy of a physically abusive home, an emotionally cold work-aholic father, a mother with an untreated mental illness, and all the chaos that followed. I've wondered why I wasn't more truant, or violent, and why I never took my own life, despite having thought about it many times. As much trouble as I did get into — drinking underage, having unprotected sex at fifteen, and running away from home — I never became trapped by my problems.

Instead, I fought back, leaving home shortly after my sixteenth birth-day, attending university with my own money, and eventually creating a family that is very different from the one in which I grew up.

Any child's life can have a fairy-tale ending, but no child is a hero who triumphs alone. I've learned from the kids that when life is hard, the secret to our success isn't just inside us. We need people and opportunities that will give us what we need to thrive. Though it's a lovely, comforting bit of popular culture to believe positive thinking is all it takes to change, real children who overcome real problems in mental health clinics, hospitals, detox centres, youth detention centres, special education programs, and all the other places they find themselves say they change when they get from us adults what they need to live less troubled lives.

Many people don't like to acknowledge this truth. They insist that if their child doesn't want to be a problem child, all he or she has to do is change. That kind of thinking makes good television but has nothing to do with what the research shows and what parents and therapists know.

This book is about children with serious problems and those at risk of them. It's about children who have a learning disability and can't read at their grade level. It's about others who are being bullied and those who steal. It's about the children who hit other children, or their parents, and those who are sexually active far too young. It's about children who are experimenting with drugs and alcohol. It's about all children who lack self-esteem.

The good news is that no matter the child's creed, colour, or capacity, every child can succeed. Children want to grow like sunflowers, tall and sturdy, with their faces pointed toward the bright light of a supportive, nurturing parent, teacher, or friend.

Trust me, I know.

It is in every child's nature to seek a less troubled life.

The Three Families

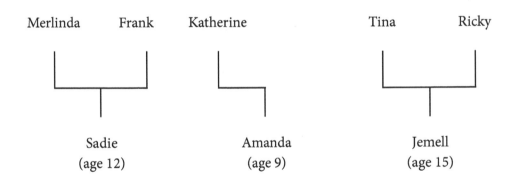

Merlinda   Frank   Katherine   Tina   Ricky

Sadie   Amanda   Jemell

(age 12)   (age 9)   (age 15)

Chapter 1

A Group for Good Parents with Difficult Kids

They were very scared when I invited them to meet as a group to talk about parenting difficult kids.

Katherine's nine-year-old daughter, Amanda, wasn't coming home after school. When she was at home, she was letting teenage boys with guns into the house while her mother was at work.

Tina and Ricky's son, Jemell, was on house arrest for assault. At fifteen, and with a learning disability that he refused to talk about, it looked certain he'd graduate from the juvenile justice system straight into a future as a career criminal.

Merlinda and Frank, meanwhile, were being outmanoeuvred by Sadie, their precocious just-turned-thirteen-year-old with a desire to get pregnant.

I am beginning to think I'm doing a pretty good job of helping them overcome their fears and tackle the chaos at home until Frank tells us he has something to say. We are just taking our seats after hanging up our coats. Tina and Ricky are sitting on the stackable chairs they've placed next to one another. Katherine is sunk into the loveseat with its tattered arms. Merlinda is leaning forward, resting on the edge of her oak armchair next to Frank. I'm in front by the flip chart, completing the tight circle we've formed.

Frank says, "Sadie is with her grandmother." His words are clipped to control his emotions. He sits with his knees apart, back straight. His posture defies us to criticize, though I'm guessing he is already beating himself up all on his own. Merlinda looks up at him, pleading for him to tell the group what she can't, or won't.

"She's there to get better. She ..." His lips twist, halfway between a gasp and a cry. He shakes one thought away and begins another. "You know, she's always been a clever kid."

No one doubts it. This is the group's eighth meeting and not the first time Frank and Merlinda have told us astonishing things about their daughter. "She's just been a bit ahead of herself," he says, his voice a little softer, more loving and protective. Merlinda reaches for his hand and we wait for Frank to tell us what's happened.

"I guess she was always a little too interested in adult things." His lips now quiver and he begins to cry. Manly tears are bled silently and wiped away quickly with the back of his hand. He surprises us when a smile passes across his face, a memory pushing aside the anguish.

"Like last year. You remember, Merlinda? The time we were in line at the drive-through. I'd ordered a tea and this sweet little voice at the other end of the intercom asks me if I'd like my bag squeezed. My God! And Sadie, she's just turned twelve years old and is sitting behind us on the way to soccer practice. Well, she starts giggling, and I'm not sure which is funnier, what the young woman just asked me or that my daughter understands why I'm blushing."

We gently laugh along with Frank, knowing full well that there are darker shadows lurking behind his smile. Sadie is likely in serious trouble.

Then Frank looks down at his big hands. He's serious now, worrying his wedding ring round and round, trying in vain to forget whatever nightmare he's living this moment. Then he rolls his shoulders up straight and looks at me, saying what he has to say loud enough for everyone to hear.

"Sadie was raped."

We all stop breathing, not believing what we're hearing, suddenly as afraid for our children's futures as we are for Sadie's. I swear I can hear Frank's heart pounding from across the room. He wrings his hands tightly, then slowly tells us. "The police have a young man in custody. He was part of the group Sadie has been hanging out with. They're all bad kids. We told Sadie to keep away from them." He shakes his head, disgusted — with the kids, maybe with himself for not having known what to do sooner.

"Sadie is threatening to kill herself if we make her come home ..." His performance breaks and he can barely speak as tears begin streaming down his face. He doesn't bother wiping them away.

We are all crying now. Tina stands and leans over Merlinda. Katherine holds her face in her hands. Even Ricky's eyes are moist. No one dares to ask Frank or Merlinda questions. Instead we all sit there, sharing their pain.

A few minutes later the silence has become unbearable. I ask the group, "Should we keep going tonight?"

It's Merlinda's turn to take charge. She pats Tina on the back, then directs her to sit down. She grabs Frank's hand and shushes him. "We came here to learn how to raise a good kid. We've had a horrible setback. But we've also had some wonderful conversations with our daughter, conversations we haven't had in years. Right now, I understand that she needs a little time to be on her own. My mom will do just fine with her. She'll feed her and let her watch all the television she wants. There will be no rules, just like Sadie likes it. I know she'll ... come ... home...." Merlinda starts to cry again, then sucks the tears back with a violent shudder, throwing her shoulders into the effort. "She'll be home ... soon."

It's brave of everyone to continue. To trust me. I have nothing certain to teach them, and yet they continue to come, hoping we can find the perfect solution that will make everything better. I say, "I have no magic tonight, but I can offer you a little hope."

Tina says, "You do that. You do whatever you can. We need to know that things get better. That's all we really need to know. Our Jemell is not doing too well, either. He's suspended, and we're worried that he's been fighting with a lot of other boys. But we know that we have to stay at it. We've got our faith still. We know he'll one day find some way of being a good boy."

There are lots of things I could talk about. The group has been using each evening meeting to talk about one of the nine foundation stones we need to put in place if we want to raise a problem-free and flourishing child. Tonight, it's thinking about hope that breaches my tongue from its cottony cocoon. I take a deep breath and dare myself to speak with authority. I want so much to help Frank and Merlinda through this evening, and the next, and the next one after that.

"Why don't we talk about what our kids need spiritually? Not just in the sense of religion — I'm talking about a sense of purpose to one's life and a sense of belonging somewhere special. Sadie will need this now more than ever."

Merlinda and Frank nod, giving me the confidence to continue. Thinking about Sadie, I ask the group, "Where did you feel you belonged as a child? At home? On your grandmother's knee? Was there a place where you felt special? We think that's home, but for many children, the kind that are likely to grow up to be problem kids, it isn't home. They think it's the street, or out among unsupervised peers. If we're lucky, those kids will find a way of connecting to a place that doesn't make their problems worse."

I look at Merlinda and Frank. They are listening, praying for answers, I'm sure. Their faces are a little softer now. We are all enjoying gentle flashbacks to warm memories of feeling embraced. I spent much of my own childhood with the chill that comes with not feeling like I belonged. It wasn't until I got into high school that I knew a sense of place where I felt safe. It was at school, running the school paper from a converted classroom. There was a sofa and a lava lamp. We could play music. I had my friends there. When class became boring, I could tell my teachers I had work to do and run to the sanctity of my hideout. I loved the quiet. It was often the janitor who reminded me I had to go home, or my stomach, rumbling for food. Only then would I reluctantly pack up my homework and drag myself home, hating the thought of what waited for me.

"I was mostly raised by my aunt," says Katherine. "My mother was a drinker."

"I had a great home," Tina tells us. "A princess bedroom all done up with frilly bedding. That sort of thing. I loved to play in there. Loved to hide in my closet among my stuffed animals. I still get all tingly thinking about it."

"Not sure I tingle," says Frank, "but I had a place. It was at church. My family made church a big deal. But I liked that. We were Baptists. There was a youth group and choir, and then later, we did other kinds of music.

I remember liking that feeling of everything being clean on Sunday."

They're all good memories. They all speak to the need we have to belong, not just to a place, but to a group of people. To sense our life as one pearl on a string, part of something bigger than ourselves. Children seem to do best when they are both needed and can make others feel needed.

I explain, "A group of peers who hangs out on the street, the kind that attracted Sadie, or a church congregation, they're a lot alike in the eyes of kids with problems."

"Wait a minute," Franks says, his voice finding its strength again. "So you're saying our kids will hang out with dangerous peers, or go to church like I did, and that there's not much difference between the two?"

"From the child's point of view, no." Frank knits his eyebrows and is about to argue. "Of course, one is better than the other but the child doesn't make the choice using the same criteria her parents use. She thinks instead, 'What's the more meaningful? Which suits me better? Which makes me feel more like I belong? Where am I a powerful little person with something to contribute?'"

Frank says, "That's how I felt at church — like someone needed me. I helped set up for special holiday celebrations. That's where my friends were. And the adults, they noticed me. I even had keys to the building when I was older."

"That's exactly it. And your family and community told you that this was something good. But what happens when a child doesn't value these things? Sometimes, problem peers are the only people, and the street the only place, where a young person feels like she belongs."

"So we leave her there?" Frank asks, sounding bitter.

"No," I reassure him, "absolutely not. But we need to know what it is about those dangerous places that makes her feel like she belongs there. Many kids living rough tell me they like the fact that their friends rely on them. That they are part of a group that gets noticed. You know the kids sitting at that busy intersection downtown, with the strange haircuts, piercings, and pit bulls tied to leashes next to them, who beg for money or squeegee windows for spare change?" Frank nods. "They like who they are. Really, they do. Though many are there because they've been chased from their homes, or fled because of abuse, they find out there on the street a sense of themselves that is, well, almost spiritual. Out there they know they belong. Maybe it's just on that corner, or in that shelter for homeless youth, but they sure feel they belong there more than at their high schools or at home or with their parents."

"That's so sad," says Tina.

"In a way. But remember, all kids want this sense of belonging and for their lives to serve some bigger purpose. Even Jemell. And Sadie, and Amanda. When we provide that to them in ways that are socially acceptable, most kid accept our invitation."

"Why would they give up their life on the street?" Merlinda asks, still dabbing at her eyes with a tissue.

"They give it up when what we are offering them is just as powerful."

"So, for Sadie ...?" Merlinda is struggling to make sense of this.

"Sadie will soon feel better — never the same, but better. But she'll be looking again for a place where she can feel connected and for a purpose to her life. If she isn't the party girl, then who will she be? If she isn't making her friends laugh or feeling like she belongs among older boys, then where will she feel the strength that comes with purpose and connection? In your home? At her school? Maybe helping her friends avoid the same thing that just happened to her."

Merlinda sits very still, not saying a word. We all take a moment to join in her silent vigil, wondering what the future holds for her hurting child and all the others we know who are just like Sadie.

Chapter 2

My Father's Cancer

On May 4, 2009, my father died of stomach cancer in Toronto. Polyps on his kidneys metastasized and spread to his other internal organs. He went from a big-bellied man with jowls and a large bald spot that he hid with a comb-over to a much thinner, sadder, hairless man with the sallow look of a cancer victim. For years my mother had yelled, "Mervyn, watch your diet!" Now I laughed to hear her harangue him with instructions to "Eat more!" Not that he had much appetite or enjoyed the feeling of food churning into acidy bile in his gut.

My father was only seventy-four when he died on a hospital ward for the terminally ill, my mother dozing in a chair near his bed. His last few days he was barely conscious. When I heard from my brother how non-communicative my father had become, I couldn't help thinking to myself, "So, what's new?" I felt guilty for thinking it but couldn't shake the secret hope that he might rally enough at the end to tell someone he missed me.

The last time we spoke was two years before his death. I had tried to phone him in the hospital after an operation to remove one of his cancerous kidneys, but my mother had refused to install a phone at his bedside. Later, my sister told me doctors had rooted around inside him for other tumours, like gardeners turning over exhausted soil in the hope of finding something else worth harvesting. When I asked my mother to connect his bedside phone, she insisted the phone was too heavy for him to hold and that I shouldn't call. That may sound crazy, but then you have to know my mother to understand she would make up any excuse to keep my father and me from speaking.

A week and a half later, my father phoned me. My brother had mentioned I'd tried to reach him. It was the first time in twenty-three years that he'd called me. The last time was when my elderly aunt, his oldest sister, died. It had struck me as odd that he broke his usual silence to tell me that. But then, it would take me some time until I understood exactly who my aunt really was.

Since my middle teens, I've known my family was odd. We were an orchestra without a conductor. There were many badly played notes that sounded more like the engine backfiring on our '68 station wagon than pleasant chatter at a dinner table. "You should ..." was usually how my mother began most sentences. My two older brothers, younger sister, and I were her audience. It was impossible for me to keep quiet. I enjoyed taunting her. "How do you know?" I'd argue, becoming more aware with each passing year that my mother hardly ever left the house. Of course, that never stopped her from offering an opinion on everything from car repairs to how to eat in a fancy restaurant. She was her own Wikipedia, with little tolerance for entries by anyone else.

I'm not proud of how I teased her, or how it drove my father to work longer hours. He'd take his dinner alone after we kids had eaten, with only my mother next to him with a half-finished cup of tea and a full plate of advice on what he could do better at work.

After I left home at sixteen, I very seldom saw my parents. Unless I phoned, they refused contact. We tumbled into an emotional abyss that lasted fifteen years until, for the sake of my children, I began having more regular contact with them. Birthdays, Mother's and Father's Day, the holidays in December, I'd phone. I took the kids to see them a few times when it was convenient. I thought my parents might like being grandparents. They didn't. My son, Scott, was fifteen, my daughter, Meg, thirteen, when my father died. He had seen them briefly three times, each visit over dinner at my brother's place a half-hour drive from their condo.

To be fair, none of this was what I was thinking about while my terminally ill father was on the phone. "How are Scott and Meg? How old are they now?" he asked. His voice was weaker than I remembered it, quivering as he pronounced my children's names. I imagined him sitting by the window of his two-bedroom condominium that overlooked a twelve-lane expressway. In the background I could hear a television blaring. A minute into our conversation, my mother called him. "Merv, your show is on." He stopped speaking for a moment. I thought I heard him exhale slowly, as if he was frustrated, or was it embarrassment? I didn't ask. I told him a little about my children, the sports they were playing and how well they were doing at school.

My father and I talked for less than ten minutes. By the time he phoned, he had long ago retired and so had practically nothing to tell me. The best he could manage was a short description of the condo where he lived and how much work it was being on the condo board. A few complaints later, we found only awkward, impenetrable silence. Eventually, he said he had to go. That he was tired and needed to rest. "Bye," he said, and for just a moment, I thought I heard his voice crack.

Thinking back to that call, it felt more like a seance than communication with my father's flesh and blood. He was an otherworldly spirit and Ma Bell, our silk-scarfed medium who momentarily connected us with her witchy ways. He never called again and I didn't attend his funeral. There was no need. "My father died many years ago," I told my best friend, Mitch, who'd known me since I was a teenager. He understood from watching my relationship stagnate for two decades that there was nothing to mourn. It made sense that I'd said my goodbyes many years earlier rather than suffer the daily insult of my father's rejection. What was the point of holding out the faint hope he might miss me when all it did was tear at my feelings and make me cranky?

When I told my kids their grandfather had died, there was a moment of quiet while we all stood looking at each other in the kitchen. I'd interrupted their evening snack to share the news.

"Should we feel sad?" Meg asked.

"No," I said. "I don't think you can really mourn someone you never knew."

"Why didn't he ever visit?" she asked.

I thought carefully about what I was about to say. There was lots I could tell them. Instead, I stuttered, "I guess, well, he was very busy. It's just too bad he never really knew what great kids you are." Meg and Scott are both sharp enough to know when I am telling them a half-truth. They'd never received birthday cards or holiday gifts from my parents. "Why would you feel anything?" I said, then worried that I sounded spiteful.

My father's death left me with a question: How did I avoid the peril of his emotional abandonment and the physical abuse that I was left to endure alone at home with my mother?

I still shudder to think about those long, angry days with her in our three-bedroom bungalow on Fredmir Street. I remember most her yelling and wheezing as she slapped me across the face or landed kicks to my backside when I didn't run away quickly enough. Worse were the times she caught me by the hair and bowled me down the hall and into my room. I dared not cry too long, or be disobedient for fear of more abuse.

I think she hated being left alone. There were long days while my father was away at work. There must have been even longer nights, judging by the collection of pornography I found in my father's bottom drawer when I was still just a boy and too young to understand what the pictures really meant.

Two weeks after my father died, I travelled to South Africa for my work. My friends in Johannesburg warned me to be careful. "Even answering your cellphone can be very dangerous. Here they won't just rob you, they'll shoot and kill you, too." The young men who do this think nothing of the consequences. Most have no education, no chance of work, and are likely HIV positive. I was relieved when we headed south from the capital, though the hopelessness that comes with staggering levels of unemployment and death seemed to cling to the people I saw through the window of our SUV.

In Bethlehem my colleagues took me to a local garbage dump where children whose parents had likely died of AIDS squatted under plastic tarps, resting while others scavenged for anything of value in the mountains of garbage. As each lorry arrived, the children swarmed, hoping to be the first to root for whatever was still of value. The children looked as dirty as the piles of refuse they stood on.

As horrible as all this sounds, what few people ever see is the orphanage two miles away where the children from the dump slept at night. Small cement rooms were carpeted with sleeping cots. A separate room provided a kitchen, and when there was enough food, a warm dinner. The centre's director said they struggle to cope with overcrowding, but it's difficult to turn a child away, especially the very young ones.

I've seen similar scenes in my own country, though the conditions are far less rank. Overcrowded foster homes with six kids in two small bedrooms of a twelve-hundred-square-foot bungalow. And yet, despite the odds, many (but not nearly enough) of these children finish school, find work, and start their own families. What is the difference that makes a difference? Why do some children thrive while others stumble?

The director of the orphanage in Bethlehem was a woman in her fifties with the roundness of a proud matriarch. She told me that all the children in her care are loved. The state gave her a little for the children who are supposed to live there. The rest, those whom she refused to turn away, are given a home because they have no other. What little surplus there was, and what charity can be had, was shared between all the children. It is the African way. A sense of community still permeated this troubled place, even if the thugs with guns forgot what their elders tried to teach them.

As we toured the compound, a small boy came over to us and stood close by the director's side. Absent-mindedly, the director's hand drifted onto his shoulder while she continued to talk about her plans to build new dormitories. I was there to explain to her about the research I was doing with my South African colleagues. My work had become an international tour of children's lives in which there is resilience amid unfathomable hardship.

It wasn't with the eye of a researcher, though, that I watched the boy nestle under the director's shadow. I was thinking about my own boyhood and how the shadow my mother cast left me cold and shivering. And how seldom my father was there to protect me.

I crouched down to stare into the boy's eyes. He stood confidently, back straight, looking at me with the calm reassurance of a child who knows his fingers are entwined in the hand of someone who will look after him. I could sense the director was looking at me now. She didn't bend down, but her eyes were there above us both. I felt just as small as that little boy. "What can you teach me?" I asked him with my eyes. "What do you know that I have yet to understand?"

Chapter 3

Three Principles

What do children need from their parents? And how do they cope when life puts them on a crash course with disaster? I have been searching for clues to the answers to these questions for years.

Until my father died, I would have said my quest was motivated 90 percent by philanthropy and 10 percent by self-discovery. These days, it feels like a more even split. Mornings, I wake with an irrepressible desire to understand why I didn't become another problem child.

On the flight home from Johannesburg, I realized I had found some answers to these questions. I couldn't quite put into words yet what I had learned, but a noisy hum at the back of my head was keeping me awake with random, disjointed thoughts. The director's hand on the boy's shoulder, the overcrowded shelter, my father dead in his hospital bed, and then a cascade of snapshots of the hundreds of children with whom I'd worked over the years. I rose and paced the aisles of the plane, trying to think about nothing, but thinking about everything instead.

By the time I landed in London, in transit for North America, I had made a decision: I would start a group for parents of children with serious problems. I'd share with them the lessons I've been taught from families like theirs all over the world. It would be a space for parents and their children to save themselves from disaster.

I'd focus the group on school-age children, but the lessons, I was sure, would also be useful to parents whose children were under five and those who had young adults camped on their couches unable, or unwilling, to get up and get on with their lives.

A week later, back in Halifax and still unsure what I should call the group or the content I'll share with parents once it begins, I head to my favourite coffee shop with a notebook and a twenty-dollar bill. It's more than enough money to keep the coffee flowing steadily, but not so much that I can hang out indefinitely. I promise myself not to leave until I've figured out what it is that makes problem children problem free and flourishing.

My first coffee is a perfect double espresso in the bottom of a heavy white ceramic cup. The coffee is whitened with a heated tumbler of frothy milk. The barista is good. As she finishes pouring the milk into the espresso, she dribbles a line across the surface of the froth, creating the impression of a leaf laid on a cloud. The first sip is warm and deliciously bitter. I can feel the synapses in my brain fire.

So, what do I know about kids, parents, problems, and solutions?

The first, and maybe the most important, thing I've learned is that *children may have problems, but they are not problem children*. Slapping a label like "problem child" on our sons and daughters does them no good whatsoever. It may even make matters worse. Children who go astray may have strange and destructive ways of coping with life's challenges, but they aren't necessarily bad kids. They hit their parents. They hit other children. They steal. They become sexually active young, very young. They get themselves into dangerous places on the Internet. They are the surly or depressive "crazies" we worry will starve themselves thin, bring knives to school, or worse, take their own lives. They are defiant, difficult children who never listen, even to good advice. And when they're really desperate, they run away, leaving us even more confused and scared than we were when we could see them acting badly in front of us.

But our children *are not their problems*. They are children first, with a keen desire to do whatever they need to do to survive this day and thrive the next. Their problems are expressions of their pain and confusion. Inside, untarnished, they remain pure little beings who start off as clean and clear of impurity as a mountain lake, the deep blue water so full of vitality you can taste it when you bend down and kiss the surface.

Children's problems Velcro to them over time. Problem behaviours become like toxins, leeching from subterranean rocks into what is otherwise pristine nature. But our children are no more their evil behaviours than a mountain lake is the heavy metals that pollute it when careless miners leave behind their toxic sludge. Help children change their behaviour, and they become as perfect as a lake that is flushed clean.

When it comes to "problem children," it is best to remember that *the problem is the problem, not the child.*

We misspeak when we say "He's a delinquent" or "She's a mischievous brat." The hyperactive, aggressive child is not just his psychiatric label but is a little boy itching for activity and an opportunity to learn.

The sexually active young teen is also a fragile young woman looking for something that she has failed to find anywhere other than in someone's bed.

The child who is homeless may be abusing drugs but is still more than the label "runaway" or "addict."

The surly seven-year-old who tells lies is still a child looking for a way to get her own way.

Thinking about all these children and their problem behaviours, I wonder, "Did I avoid becoming a delinquent because I found other ways to cope with the rejection and abuse I experienced?" It's certainly plausible. I never felt like a bad kid *inside*, even though I often heard that most everything about me was bad.

One cappuccino down, I can feel the group taking shape. The women at the table beside me keep glancing my way. I think I may have being talking to myself, imitating the Count from *Sesame Street*. "One, ah, ah, ah!" They don't look like they have kids or see anything funny in a single guy acting childish. I order a second coffee and sip it slowly, waiting for inspiration.

Thoughts about childhood television remind me of my favourite show when I was a kid. *The Six Million Dollar Man* was a series begun in 1974 that proudly announced at the start of each episode, "We have the tech-nology...." I would watch that show with my brothers on the sofa in the rec room downstairs. There was never any of our regular squabbling when the show came on. Even my father occasionally sat down to watch it with us, though he was more likely to fall asleep after dinner in his La-Z-Boy upstairs. If we were especially good, my mother might let us set up folding tables and watch the show while we ate.

Maybe that's it. That's the second principle. *We have the technology.* When it comes to children with problems, I am convinced we have what it takes to help every one of them succeed. Whether the child is a small boy in a South African township or a girl living in a middle-class North American suburb, we know what to do to ensure that children grow up well. There is more than enough research to convincingly show us that *a well-cared-for child will grow up well.*

The children I work with have shown me that when the adults around them provide what they need to change from swirling masses of problems to competent, caring contributors to their families and communities, kids change for the better. The research is very clear on this point. With the right support, the vast majority of children will succeed and do well enough to become invisible to social workers, police, mental health specialists, addic-tions counsellors, and even school vice-principals (who always seem to have the responsibility of dealing with the problem kids).

You may have heard that individuals have to want to change in order for change to happen. In fact, that's turned out to be just a lot of psy-chobabble that blames kids for being left to figure things out for them-selves. The truth is that children are much like the tomato plants in my neighbour's garden. She could just toss the seeds and hope for the best, but she doesn't. If she did, she knows that she'd be lucky to get a few scrawny plants. Of course, those few plants would eventually bear fruit and we'd likely be in awe of how hardy, resilient, or just plain lucky they are. Instead, she takes the time to ensure the soil is ready for the seed-lings, with the right nutrients tomatoes need. Then she stakes each plant to ensure the fragile stems aren't broken and that there's enough sunlight to make the fruit ripen. Judging by her crop, almost every single plant thrives whether it is motivated to produce fruit or not.

It would be strange to talk about those vulnerable plants needing positive thinking to grow. They thrive because of what is provided to them. Gardeners are a lot like parents, educators, grandparents, coaches, and whoever else is present in a child's life.

There's no better way to prove this than to look at what happened to the hundreds of thousands of Romanian orphans who were abandoned in state institutions. Two years after the Communist leader Nicolae Ceausescu took power in 1965, all forms of contraception were made illegal. Ceausescu was intent on increasing Romania's population by 50 percent in ten years. The result was huge families living in poverty, with no solution but to abandon to state orphanages the children they couldn't feed. By the early 1980s, Ceausescu was trying to repay foreign debt by starving social programs, creating deplorable, inhumane conditions for the orphans. There was little food, widespread physical and sexual abuse, and strict discipline. Worse, those who toured the orphanages reported four to five babies to a crib, or children raised for years in windowless basements, their eyes having never seen daylight. Many children were never held. They lacked the stimulation that is required to grow healthy brains and the cuddling that teaches children how to form emotional bonds with others.

As late as 2001, as many as three thousand Romanian children a year were being placed in international adoptions with families in countries like Britain, the United States, Canada, and Australia. No surprise, many of these children showed serious developmental delays, unable to play, learn, or attach to their parents. Those who were adopted before age two showed the least damage and were the ones most likely to bounce back. For those fortunate enough to be adopted after age two, the chances of a full recovery were remote.

Sir Michael Rutter and his colleagues in Britain took the time to follow more than a hundred Romanian adoptees over eleven years. The good news is that all children, no matter what their early experience of deprivation, can improve when they are given the right kind of support from parents, special educators, speech language pathologists, and a flotilla of child psychiatrists, psychologists, and other therapists.

The strange thing is, though, that the children who had been the most deprived, who had been orphans the longest and who had the most severe problems, continued to improve quickly for all eleven years. They were given lots of supports like teachers' aides in their classrooms once they went to school. Unexpectedly, the Romanian orphans who were less deprived showed much slower rates of improvement *after* they began elementary school.

Why the difference? It had little to do with the children and everything to do with what happened when they entered grade one. Only the neediest of children were given the extra help at school. The relatively normal, but still developmentally delayed kids, were left to self-repair. The special educators who had worked with them earlier in their lives seemed to be saying, "We've done enough. Even though you still have potential to improve much more, we can no longer give you the extra help you need." That left parents to fill in for the social service providers who were told to walk away.

Clearly, when it comes to helping children with severe problems, we know what to do, but that doesn't mean we always do everything we should. Even when we know we are falling short of expectations, we still sometimes hold back, willing to pay later for problems we could have fixed much earlier.

If I'm going to hold a group for parents, it's going to need more than two guiding principles. What else do I know? For the moment nothing comes to mind except daydreams from my troubled past.

There was a period of time when I wouldn't have felt like I belonged in a trendy café drinking cappuccinos. I would have preferred bars, or the back seats of cars, or the basements of friends' homes as places to gather my thoughts and enjoy the chaos of risk-taking and rule-breaking. If what we experience when we're younger sows the seeds for the kind of adult we become, then I should have a drinking problem and have fathered a child before I was ready to support it.

Growing up in Montreal in the 1970s, I could sneak into bars with a fake ID. My buddies and I drove around on mopeds after dark, throwing eggs at strangers, or followed police cruisers to see what kind of trouble we could find. None of it landed me in detention, but I lived close enough to the line that I'm surprised I didn't find myself in lock-up at least once.

My parents never knew even a tenth of what I was up to. By day, I maintained good grades, but in the evenings, beyond their front door, I let my anger and recklessness take over. My greatest regret was almost fathering a child when I was just fifteen. Too shy to buy condoms, my girlfriend and I did what we could to avoid her getting pregnant but there was an anxious three months when we weren't sure if she was. Weeks ticked by. I argued more at home. It was hard to think straight at school. And all the while, we both waited for something to tell us we would be okay. It was one of many scares that kept reminding me that there was more danger than I imagined at my doorstep.

I don't believe our past has to predict our future. Still, I won't lie. I've responded to my own children's misbehaviour under the shadow of my past. I'm ashamed to say I've given my children a hurtful squeeze or a heavy push onto a bed, and raised my voice so loud it shook doors. I've worried at how close I've come to calling them names, or worse, becoming cold and indifferent toward them like my father was to me. Thankfully, I've had the good sense to know when to shut the door or go for a walk to calm down, always with the mantra in my head, "I'm not like my parents."

So why didn't I self-destruct? Repeat the cycle of abuse? Allow myself to become another problem child?

I order a third cup of coffee, this time a single espresso, and stare out the window at the traffic. It's still early evening but the streets are jammed. Hardly anyone walks anymore. I can count to ten between pedestrians who by happenstance stroll by the plate-glass window. All the while the traffic hums like a throbbing headache.

An hour later, I order a fourth espresso. I've written nothing. The waitress checks her watch as she takes the order. When she brings me my drink, I'm still staring out the window, thinking as much about what I see on the street as my search for principles for good parenting. Two middle-aged women stop to say hello on the sidewalk in front of me. They are carrying cloth shopping bags and laughing at something one of them tells the other. That's nice, I think. For a moment it occurs to me that if we're going to decongest our city streets, it's not enough that people stop driving. We have to start walking, too.

Maybe raising great kids is the same. We spend so much effort getting them to *stop* doing bad things that we forget that what saves them from their problems is giving them opportunities to show us what great kids they can be. One could say that children should be *problem free and flourishing*. That's it! I'm totally buzzing with caffeine but am sure that's the third principle.

Successful people don't just suppress problems, they build capacity. I want my children to do good things in the world, for themselves and others. I want them to build their self-esteem, show others their talents, be kind, and grow up to be good citizens. I want them to understand other people's rights, act responsibly, and promote equality. I want them to find ways, big and small, to make the world a better place.

These wishes are very different things from arguments with a child to stop talking back to his teachers, stop yelling in the grocery store, stop using drugs, stop running away, or stop failing in school. If I can stop those behaviours, I can raise a child who is problem free. Then what? I don't just want a shy, withdrawn child who sits in his room, never talking to anyone, never asserting himself, never making the world a better place with his smile and talents. Being problem free is not at all the same thing as flourishing.

If I break my leg snowboarding and am in a cast, I'll be forced to hobble around on crutches for months. That doesn't mean I can't still hold down a job, develop great relationships, think of myself as someone who matters, or celebrate my many talents (other than snowboarding, of course). In other words, despite the emotional and physical scars we carry with us, we can still demonstrate to others that we are wonderful people with a contribution to make.

That's what resilience is really about. It's about what we do even when the scars of the past are there beneath our clothes.

Are three principles enough? *There are children with problems, but they are not problem children; a well-cared-for child will grow up well; and children need to be problem free and flourishing.* They're a good place to start.

I pay my bill (eighteen dollars with tax and a three-dollar tip!) and go home. As I walk, I think of names for the group. There's no contest. It's got to be the Last Problem Child. Except, it won't be a group that just ends children's problems. It will also help parents give their children everything they need to enjoy lifelong success.

Chapter 4

Three "Problem" Children

Sadie looks like a stiff breeze could blow her over. When I first meet her, she's only twelve, but already she's committed to looking like a vampire. Pasty white skin accented by black eyeliner to go with the jet-black colour she's dyed her previously reddish-blond hair. Her jeans are black. Her T-shirt has the red-scar splash of an Emo band logo I don't recognize. She smiles at me when we meet. She had insisted her mother wait outside while we spoke.

Everyone is worried she's anorexic. Or suicidal. Maybe both. She wears thick leather wristbands that work well to hide the scars that have formed over the cuts she inflicted on herself with a razor. There are also scars on her stomach and thighs, according to her mother, whom I spoke with on the phone. What strikes me most, though, when I meet Sadie, is that she's smiling. A big, wide, toothy grin. There's no malice. She's more greyhound than pit bull despite the studded leather trim on the short coat she wears. She weighs just ninety pounds. Her mother worries Sadie will be kidnapped, picked up and carried away by some street youth, like the ones Sadie likes to chat up when she's on her way to the mall.

"My mother doesn't understand anything about me," Sadie says. "I don't cut myself any more. It was just a few times and only when she was screaming at me. I keep telling her I'm okay, I'm eating. I'm just really into my own kind of fashion. But she worries." Sadie sounds angry at first, then her tone changes and she lets her shoulders slump. "Everyone worries," she says.

"Is that something we could work on? Getting your mom to worry less?"

"Yeah, that would be okay. And my stepdad, too. He's mostly all right, but they really don't understand. Not me, or my friends. We're not bad kids. And no one is going to kidnap me and take me away and rape me or anything like that."

Her description of such violence catches me out. I didn't expect her to be quite so aware of everything her parents were worrying about. "I guess they don't think you can handle things yourself. If I'm understanding them, it's like you're a china doll. Really fragile."

"That's it exactly. But I'm not stupid like they think. My friend told me to try the cutting, that it would help with all the hassles at home. But it didn't really. Maybe for a little, but then it meant going to see doctors and missing school, and my parents have been completely freaked. Now they really hate my friends. It's way too much hassle to try that shit again."

"So how would you like your parents to see you? If you're not a problem child needing their protection."

"I'm not fragile, you know. I'm really strong even if I don't look it. And I'm very unique. I listen to music that most of the kids at school have never heard of. Really alternative stuff. I'd get a tattoo, too, but my folks won't let me. But I can do some piercings if I keep it reasonable." I notice she wears six studs in one ear, four in the other. She has a nose ring, too. I'll admit the thought of creating large, round holes in my ears, or sticking pins through the more tender parts of my lips, tongue, eyebrows, or places I keep hidden seems more like ritualistic abuse than fun. But then I had my own crazy way of expressing my individuality as a kid. Sadie has hers.

It takes a few meetings, but Sadie eventually agrees to let me meet with her and her mother in the same room. Her stepfather, Frank, isn't invited. In the weeks leading up to that meeting, Sadie has stopped cutting, and she's eating. She's not running away, either. In return for not worrying her parents, Sadie's managed to get her mother to lighten up a little on the rules. Sadie is again walking to the mall with her friends. And she's planning to attend a big outdoor concert in a few weeks.

It sounds good, but when Sadie's mother, Merlinda, joins us, Sadie reverts to the argumentative child she is at home. She slouches in her seat, thrusting her hands into the pockets of her skin-tight jeans. She mumbles her words and says "I don't know" to most questions. I'm beginning to understand why her mother doesn't trust her daughter. There's nothing very mature about a moody twelve-year-old acting like she's two again.

Merlinda has gone grey early. Her shoulder-length hair is pulled back tight into a short braid. She sits with her hands clasped between her legs, her two feet firmly on the floor. You have to look closely to see the tiny crow's feet wrinkling the corners of her eyes. Maybe it's her work that keeps her young. She's a physiotherapist who specializes in rehabilitating patients who have suffered traumatic brain injuries after car accidents. It must be difficult, I think to myself, for her to be as optimistic about her own daughter's ability to heal, even with her help.

Merlinda leans forward to speak, pivoting at the hips, her hands tightly knotted in front of her. "She was a lovely child but I worry all the time about her. We're letting her go to the concert. I know how much she wants to go, but really, look at her. Someone could just pick her up and steal her away and she's not going to be able to do anything to stop it from happening."

Sadie just rolls her eyes and slides lower in her chair. She's not looking at me any longer. She's looking at the floor, then the door. I know I'm losing her. What child wants to be told she's as fragile as a teddy bear and just as mindless? But then again, her mother has a right to worry. Sadie's grades have slipped. There are the marks on her wrists, and her weight is precariously low.

It's difficult for Merlinda to see what Sadie sees when she looks in the mirror: an artistic fashionista with an ear for music and the stick-it-in-your-face personality of a kick-ass grrrl. Femininity with a growl. I'll admit that the more I get to know Sadie, the more I admire her. But then, I wasn't the one who had to spend time in a hospital emergency room with my child's wrists tightly wrapped in blood-soaked gauze.

"I've lightened up the rules for now, but we'll see if things change," says Merlinda.

Thinking about her willingness to trust her daughter again, I'm left wondering if Merlinda might not be able to help teach other parents how to do the same. A week later I call her. "Would you and your husband consider joining a few other families in a group? I've been thinking that you might have some great advice for other parents, and maybe they could offer you some support with Sadie. If you agree, I'll keep seeing Sadie alone, or with you, but the group will be a special place just for the adults."

"You really think talking to other parents would help?"

"Actually, I was thinking that what you're dealing with, and how you're dealing with it, might be useful for other people to hear. You can share as much or as little as you like. I'll present each evening a little about raising kids — things I've learned over the years — then we'll learn from each other. How's that sound?"

Merlinda isn't sure, but she says she'll talk to her husband, Frank. He holds a senior position in the department of the environment. "I'm not sure if he has the time," she says.

"It will be just one evening a week," I say, trying to make the group seem less intimidating, but also desperate to find my first family.

A few days later, Merlinda calls me back. She sounds tired but says they're interested. "Anything we can do to help Sadie, we're willing to try." I promise to get back to her as soon as I have found the other families.

"Tomorrow wouldn't be soon enough," she sighs.

"Has something happened since we last met?" I ask, taking the cue.

She begins to sob. "She posted pictures of herself on the Internet. With her top pulled up." She can barely speak through the tears. "I heard about it from the principal.... He overheard kids teasing her. What are we going to do with her?"

"I'm sorry, really sorry, to hear this."

"Why is she doing this? Why?"

I don't have an easy answer. "It will take time to explain, Merlinda. But not too much time."

The next day, I am still feeling unsettled about Sadie and the dangerous path she is following. I have to park those thoughts, though, while I introduce myself to Tina and Ricky, parents to five children ages five to fifteen. Their oldest, Jemell, is proving to be a dangerous handful in ways quite different from Sadie. A black boy growing up in a mostly white community, he's been the target of racial slurs since he was little. The more he fights back, the more his teachers, the police, and social workers watch him. Tina and Ricky aren't just worried about Jemell. Their other children are doing well at school and so active playing sports in the evenings that the inside of their minivan looks like a mobile compost bin. They like the chaos but are wondering if all their kids will turn out to be as troubled as Jemell despite their good starts.

Jemell's behaviour would put any family on edge. He was overheard by one of his teachers threatening a younger boy in the bathroom with circumcision unless he gave Jemell his lunch money. Jemell insists he was joking, but the child wet himself and ran screaming straight to the principal, who called the police. Jemell had threatened to slit the principal's throat before the police wrestled him to the ground and, with hundreds of students listening behind locked classroom doors, hog-tied and carried him out to a cruiser. He was found guilty of a number of crimes and sentenced to house arrest for six months. He was also expelled, meaning he has to attend a special school for delinquents.

"He's been like that now for a few years," Tina tells me and starts crying. She's a stout woman whose toes barely touch the ground when she sits up straight in an office chair. She's wearing a brightly coloured blouse that reminds me of somewhere more exotic and warm. Ricky, who has the squat, muscular shape of a weightlifter, puts a thick hand over hers. It feels like he's protecting her from me. I choose my words carefully.

"Please tell me more."

Tina keeps wiping her eyes, leaving me to count through the silence. I get to twenty-three before Ricky saves us. "He got picked on a lot," he explains. "There aren't many black families where we live, and Jemell, he was the first kid in the school who was different. We told him to fight back when other kids beat him up. But we never thought he'd become the one starting the fights."

Tina blows her nose into a tissue she pulls from a box on the table between us. "I'm not sure what he needs. We've tried more rules, but he just keeps breaking them. And he's smoking weed. We know that. And there are the girls. Despite everything, we agreed to take him home on house arrest."

"A boy like Jemell is only going to learn bad things in jail," Ricky adds, perhaps trying to convince himself that he and Tina are up to the task of being Jemell's jailers. They must, I'm guessing, be wondering how they'll ever keep a close enough watch over their eldest son. Tina works as an office administrator for a bank, Ricky is a customs inspector on the docks. The children's grandparents help with after-school routines until Tina can get home and make dinner or Ricky can bundle their brood into the van and fight traffic to get to one of the many sports fields that ring the city. It's unlikely two seniors are going to be able to keep control of an aggressive teenager whose mission in life is to have his own way.

I reassure Tina and Ricky that they aren't to blame for what's happened. In fact, I admire what they've done for their family. The challenge will be to figure out how to get Jemell to change course before he ends up in an adult facility doing serious time.

"He's got a learning disability, too, you know. It means he doesn't do well when he has to read a lot. But he won't go for extra help. God knows we've tried to make him go." Tina starts to cry again; her tears are silent rivers down her cheeks. Ricky hands her the box of tissues.

"Jemell is like a couple of his uncles that way," Ricky says. "I've done fine, but Jemell's uncles are more likely to be crooks than cops." He shakes his head and it's Tina's turn to put her hand over his.

"How did you not repeat the pattern?" I ask.

"I just saw what it was doing to everyone. I'm no chickenshit — I don't back down from a fight — but I wasn't going to piss my life away like they did. Funny, but my father doesn't always think much of what I do. He made a lot of money in some pretty crooked real estate deals. Took a lot of poor people's money. It wasn't quite stealing but damn close. I think the way Tina and I live embarrasses him. Like I should be doing even better if I'm all legit. It's Tina's folks who help with the kids." I nod, realizing that Ricky and I have more in common than I might have guessed looking at his life from the outside.

"So you decided to do things differently?"

"I had to. Or else it was jail." He stops speaking as he wrings his hands together with a tremendous force, bulging the muscles under his long-sleeved shirt. "I can't let that happen to Jemell. Not after everything I went through to get here."

As we wrap up for the day, I'm pretty sure I've found my second family.

With two families willing to try the group, I ask my colleagues for referrals for more. A few families prefer to work with me one-on-one. I respect that and don't push. Ten days later, though, I meet Katherine and her daughter Amanda. Katherine could use some support and I sense I could learn a lot from her as well. She's had a difficult life, and her nine-year-old daughter isn't making things any easier. Katherine is in her late thirties, though the black circles beneath her eyes and grey steaks in her hair make her look ten years older. She doesn't seem very comfortable sitting in my office either, having squeezed her ample hips between the two fixed arms of a narrow office chair. I make a note to have a more comfortable chair for her the next time she visits. Amanda sits in the chair next to her, a stocky child with a double chin and glasses. Her father, Katherine's second husband, died of an aneurysm two years earlier. Amanda must have inherited her darker complexion and oval black eyes from him. Katherine has one older daughter whom she had when she was still a teenager. They don't see each other very much. That leaves Katherine alone a great deal and at the mercy of Amanda's wild tantrums.

Not that Amanda is always at home. She's already been placed twice in a special group home for children with severe behavioural problems. She's home now, with a list of things that Katherine is supposed to do to help her daughter with her anger and impulsivity. Their family doctor thinks Amanda has attention deficit hyperactivity disorder and a variety of other problems that carry similarly long names. But the school psychologist has yet to provide a full assessment.

"I'm at my wits' end knowing how to get her to behave and go to school when she's supposed to go," Katherine tells me. She sounds panicked and short of breath, her words wheezy and sad.

Amanda picks at her hangnails, chewing on one thumb then the other. She wears black spandex pants, which look terribly odd on a nine-year-old but I'm guessing are comfortable or warm, maybe both. "And don't get me started on her choice of clothes or getting her to comb her hair or take a shower. She won't do anything I tell her to do. Nothing!"

Before I can ask Amanda a question, Katherine notices Amanda about to take off her coat. "You'd better keep your jacket on," she says. "It's cold in here with the air conditioning. You'll catch a cold, and then you'll be my problem." I'm not surprised when Amanda unzips the coat and tosses it on an empty chair. Then she flicks her greasy hair and stares defiantly back at her mother, snapping the spandex on her thighs.

"And you, Amanda, what do you think? About the problems at home?"

She shrugs and looks at my shoes, then twists her head around and stares at the paper clips on my desk. She reaches for the magnetic holder and begins to string them together. I wait. When Katherine tries to fill the empty space, I raise a finger, a subtle hint to just wait a while longer.

"She knows," Amanda says.

"Sorry? She knows what?"

"What I feel. She's always telling me what to do and what I think. She knows."

I'm pretty sure Katherine doesn't know what it feels like to be a distractible nine-year-old or feel stupid because you can't do your school work. There's not a lot of other places for Amanda to go to find something good to say about herself, either. The family lives in a subsidized housing project that would have looked worn and tattered twenty years ago when it was middle-aged. Unlike a lot of her neighbours, though, Katherine holds a part-time job. She's a translator. Though she grew up on the prairies, her mother was Ukrainian and her Russian is pretty good. She dreams, she tells me, of moving to another part of the city where there's less crime. But she doesn't have the money. She has never liked her neighbours, who she says are thieves and murderers. Amanda, every bit the drama queen, throws her arms into the air and shouts, "Mom! You can't say that. They probably think the same about you."

"Do you like where you live?" I ask Amanda.

"Yeah." She won't tell me why. I'm guessing she feels less pressure to go to school among the other disadvantaged kids she lives beside than the kids in the suburban townhouses she walks by on the way to school.

"But Mom is crazy. That's what the problem is. It's her, not me." I raise an eyebrow. What I soon learn is that Amanda means her mother likes her house tidy. Towels nicely folded and stacked in the closets. Shoes arranged in pairs by the front door. Dishes washed and put away before going to bed. Nothing out of the ordinary, except if you're nine years old and live beside people who are having trouble getting out of bed most mornings or seeing to it that their children do the simple things like brush their teeth or go to school every day.

"Well," confides Katherine, "that's just how I cope. There were some pretty crazy times for all of us when Amanda was younger. I went through a pretty awful depression after my first husband left me. I did some things I'm not too proud of. Things to prove I could make it on my own." I'm not sure I'm understanding, so I sit and wait. "I was with a lot of men for a time. I did anything I had to do for money. I was even an exotic dancer. That kind of thing. I think it embarrasses Amanda."

Amanda doesn't look the least bit embarrassed. In fact, she looks confident that I'll now fully appreciate which of them is the saner one. I reserve all judgments and instead invite Katherine to attend the group. Amanda asks if she'll have to attend, too.

"No, it's mostly for your mom, but we may have some sessions you can attend. Would you do that?"

"If you can make my mom less weird, then maybe."

Katherine is about to explode but instead swallows hard. "Let's meet individually next time," I say and they both finally relax.

"As long as it's not too long from now," Katherine says and glares at Amanda.

"It shouldn't be. Is there some hurry?"

"You want to tell him?" she asks her daughter, her tone pleasant like the shiny, mottled skin of an unripe apple that reveals its bitterness when you foolishly bite.

"It wasn't my fault," Amanda protests.

When I continue to look confused, Katherine explains, "She let a boy in our house. A boy who has a gun. I saw the gun. It's real, no matter what Amanda says. I haven't phoned the police. Yet." I wait for an explanation. "I have to live next to that family. But I've told Amanda she can have nothing to do with that boy. And he can't come in my house."

"It wasn't a real gun!" Amanda screams.

"That's what she says," Katherine says, ignoring her daughter. "We'll see. That boy is going to get himself in big trouble. Already has from what I hear. But it won't be in my house." Amanda rolls her eyes and our time is up. We have a lot of work to do. And soon. Both Katherine and I agree the group will be a perfect and well-timed support.

With three families now committed, I can start. I phone back Tina and Ricky, and Merlinda and Frank. We decide Tuesday evenings work best. Within a week, I find myself in a room with five parents eager to fix their kids. I hope I can deliver on my promise to help them. To be truthful, I doubt I can really fix anyone, kid or adult. I can, I figure, offer them some hope, and a safe space to share what I'm learning from families like theirs.

Little did I realize who the real teachers would be, and who would be the student.

Chapter 5

The Last Problem Child Group Begins

It's early October and raining the evening we begin the group. Fall gusts have whooshed leaves into piles by the curb. The trees are enjoying one last glorious strut, shaking their bounty, before winter settles them to bed. The rain turns the leaves into smudges of wet crimson and gold that are trampled underfoot. Fall for me is a time of warm sweaters and hot cups of tea. The furnace kicking on for the first time and sleeping snug in a warm bed next to an open window. It's like camping beside a high mountain lake, only with a thermostat and an electric kettle at the ready once I get brave enough to put my feet back on the cold floor.

By the time evening rolls around, I've already had a hectic day except I'm not tired in the least. All day I floated above the endless stream of meetings and phone calls that needed to be made, my mind on the first few minutes of the upcoming group.

I've borrowed a room at a local treatment centre for street youth where I work part-time. The setting is ideal. The room is in a suite of offices above a small family-owned business on the border between three different neighbourhoods. To the north are squat, working-class homes now becoming gentrified as housing prices rise quickly. To the east are older streets full of rundown townhouses and flats, with a couple of subsidized housing projects that carry nicknames like the Project and the

Square. To the west and south are middle-class families living in their own fully detached homes on treed lots. Doctors live alongside artists, students, and accountants. In their basement apartments are young people who work in the bars and coffee shops downtown.

The meeting room has comfortable couches and a coffee table. There's a kitchen open to a great room and an old coal fireplace that doesn't work. The woodwork is distressed but has been left unpainted. The aged mahogany gives one the impression that some things endure even if you don't take good care of them.

Sadie's parents arrive first. Merlinda keeps her coat on and takes a seat close to the door. Frank is here, too. I introduce myself. "Hello," he says and we extend our hands to one another at the same moment. His handshake, when we grip, is cautious at first, then overly firm. I doubt he wants to be here. I ask about Sadie. "She's at home tonight," Merlinda tells me, "with the computer locked away in our bedroom. She told us she wouldn't leave the house. That's a nice change." I nod and decide to leave it at that. There will be time to talk later about change and whether locking computers away from twelve-year-olds is really the solution to a young woman's precocious interest in sex.

Ricky opens the door and thunders in with Tina behind him. "I don't know why you can't park closer. It's raining. You could have dropped me at the door." Tina says all this to Ricky before they've even sat down. She rolls her eyes and curses "men" beneath her breath. But she's all smiles for me. Tonight at least, I'm an exception to a rule.

Katherine shows up at a minute to seven. I was beginning to wonder if she'd be here. She's flustered as she comes in. Ricky points to where she can leave her coat. She shakes the rain from it, then spreads it over a chair to dry. She sits herself primly on the sofa I've placed in among a crescent of less comfortable stacking chairs, like those in my own office. Katherine's hands clasp both shoulders while she rubs herself warm.

"Should I turn up the heat?"

"No, I'll be fine." She smiles. "I'm always cold. That's what Amanda is always telling me. Hates it when I keep the house warm. Complains I'm not being green. It's not like we pay for the oil." Katherine loses her smile. "I mean, our heat comes with the place. It's included." She isn't going out of her way to tell the other families she lives in subsidized housing. In fact, from the sad expression now on her face, I think she's pleading with me to keep her secret. Merlinda smiles warmly at the explanation. "I wish I could say the same," and we all join in a very adult-like nod. I'm guessing everyone appreciates a night away from the kids.

"It's good that you all could come." I can feel my breath catch in my chest. As I sit in front of them, I feel like an imposter. They are looking toward the front of the room for answers when, in truth, everything I've ever learned about raising great kids has come from the kids themselves and their families. I want to change seats. Actually, I want to sit on the floor and let them lecture me. Wouldn't that freak them out.

Instead, I force air deep into my lungs, contract my diaphragm, and then lunge upward, an expulsion of air and self-doubt all in one. I'm ready to begin.

We do introductions and sign confidentiality agreements. Fill up cups of tea and coffee in the kitchen. When we're all settled, I ask each of them to tell the group what they most want to learn. I'm not surprised when Ricky says he wants to know how to better control Jemell, and Frank nods vigorously. Merlinda shyly says she wants to know Sadie still loves her. Katherine looks like she's going to cry. Tina laughs at Merlinda's wish. "Love me? I just want my Jemell to get out of bed and not fight at school. I want him to respect me. Love, I know he loves me. He's my son. But respect, I ain't so sure."

"That's a good place to start," I say and remind them that we'll meet ten more times after tonight. Respect and love will both be discussed often. Tonight, though, is just an introduction. I tell them they can challenge me anytime. Ask any questions they like.

"Anything?" asks Katherine.

"Anything." I repeat the word with more emphasis this time and Katherine settles into a more comfortable position on the sofa.

I begin, as I will most evenings, by telling them a story. My first one is about hope and the invincible spirit of a remarkable child. That's what you think of when you meet Thabo. He's fourteen and HIV positive. His parents and grandparents are all dead from AIDS. Post-apartheid South Africa, his home, is a place where HIV has infected at least a quarter of the population and likely more. Thabo lives in a northern tin-roofed slum with his elder sister and three cousins. The road he walks to school, when he feels well enough to go, is so badly potholed even medical staff often have to walk to their clinic, leaving their Land Rovers and drivers at the edge of the settlement. At night they leave. They have to. The community is a tangle of street criminals and gangs that terrorize those who can't afford to live anywhere else: the chronically unemployed — with only a year, or maybe two, of formal schooling — pregnant teenagers with their first-born already slung across their hips, and glue-sniffing elders who sit in comatosed heaps staring into the street. Amid this despair, Thabo walks freely, often late into the night, searching for someone to feed him.

Something ignites hope in the boy. Perhaps it's because he knows he's good at school. And he likes his teachers as much as they like him. He also likes to play chess, and when he's eaten, enjoys a game of soccer with his friends, of which he has many. They play with a tattered, half-inflated ball, barefoot on a patch of dirt next to piles of garbage. They practise moves that they've watched on staticky old televisions people have rescued from the dump. Life's okay, Thabo says, if he has food and medicine. Thankfully, the retrovirals he needs to keep his immune system working are available at the free clinic.

As he wanders his community, you can see that he feels connected to this impoverished place where everyone knows Thabo and his story. It would be nice if he had one special caregiver who smiled at him before he went to sleep each night, but Thabo has only memories of such intimacy. Perhaps those memories are enough for now. He contents himself instead by staying woven into the fabric of a village. There is an African proverb that says, "If you want to walk fast, walk alone; if you want to walk far, walk with others." Thabo has chosen to walk far.

No matter what we build over it — a temple or an outhouse — the foundation stones for a happy, healthy child are still the basics like food, security, a place in one's community, and — when it's available — some-one's love. Individual motivation to survive is only a small part of what keeps Thabo alive.

"If we do our part as their parents, teachers, and community elders, then most of our children are going to do all right," I explain to the group, wondering if an AIDS orphan in an African slum was a poor choice of subject matter for a story. I think it's easier, though, to see things when we're pushed from our comfort zones. "I was hoping the story would offer you hope. Remind you that kids can come through even the worst of situations and still do fine. *If we do our part as responsible caregivers.*"

"Are you saying my Sadie is like Thabo?" Merlinda looks unconvinced. "I don't think so."

My head begins to pound as creeping self-doubt blankets me. First group, first activity, and all I can hear is a voice saying, "You're a failure, dummy." I frown and push the negative thoughts aside.

"If I had told you a story about a child from here, maybe one of your children, then every other parent in the room could say, 'That's not my child.' Thabo is, well, not your children. And yet, he is a child all the same. That means he needs the same things your kids need. And, of course, your kids need the same things he needs."

"I think I get what you're trying to say. A little," says Ricky. Taking a deep breath, he tries to explain himself to the group. "My son Jemell isn't a bad kid beneath it all. Tina and me, we know that. So, you're saying he's looking for something and is messing up badly while doing his looking."

"I know it's difficult to imagine that we could overlook what our kids need," I continue. "We're their parents, after all. We're expected to know them inside out. But I'll tell you, the closer we are to our children, the more we see them the way we want to see them: as pint-sized versions of ourselves. We think they need only what we think they need, in ways that make sense to us, not to them."

"So you think our Sadie has all these problems because she isn't getting from us what she needs?" Frank asks, his tone defensive.

"What do you think?" I ask, not wanting to fall into the trap of being the group know-it-all.

Merlinda jumps in. "Sadie has food and medicine and isn't treated badly. I'll bet that child in Africa would love to have Sadie's life."

She may be right, though I bet there are things about Sadie's life, and Jemell's and Amanda's, that Thabo wouldn't want. "I think Sadie needs lots of things from you, including rules and expectations that she follows them." Frank smiles and relaxes a little. "But she also needs lots of other things, too."

I go to the flip chart and lift the first piece of paper. On the next sheet, I've written in my best handwriting the three principles that I'm basing the group on. "I know that no two children are alike, but I have learned that if I'm going to help them, or better yet, if *we* are going to help them, it's easier if we think about them and their problems with these three points in mind." I read from the flip chart:

- There are children with problems, but they are not problem children.
- A well-cared-for child will grow up well.
- Children need to be problem free and flourishing.

A little shy, I tell them about my favourite coffee shop and how I came up with each point.

Katherine asks, "So you're saying if we keep these points in mind, our children will do all right?"

"Yes and no. These are just principles that I use to keep my head on straight. When I met each of your children, I kept reminding myself that these are wonderful young people with great potential despite their problem behaviours. That's point one. And I reminded myself that there is lots of wisdom out there, and within each of you, that I can tap to help your children grow up well and find everything they need to succeed. That's point two. Finally, I kept in mind that my job wasn't just to get Amanda to come home after school, Sadie to change her peer group, or Jemell to be less delinquent. It was also to help you as families help your children realize their potential to be wonderful, flourishing young people in a world that is complex and sometimes dangerous. That's point three."

"I get all that," says Ricky. "But what's next? What do we actually *do* to help our kids? It's all fine to see them as great kids, and to know they have potential, but how do we help them stop being problem children?"

"And turn them into the nice boys and girls we want them to be," adds Merlinda.

"This group may be based on these three principles," I explain, "but we're not going to talk about them much. Instead, I want to explore what children actually need to make them problem free and flourishing. The principles will remain in the background, reminding us that there needn't be any more problem children." They look satisfied with what I've just said. Now, it will just take time to share with them what I've learned from families like theirs.

"Children like Thabo, and the hundreds of others that I've worked with and spoken to right here in this community, have taught me that our kids need nine things to stop their problem behaviours and to flourish. I thought we'd talk about one each evening that we meet. Tonight, though, I want to start with what *you* know, instead of what I know. I think you'll be surprised to discover that you know lots of exceptionally important things about raising children."

"Wait," says Katherine, seeming a little bored. "You're not going to tell us these nine magical things tonight? You're going to make us wait?" She looks at Merlinda and Frank for support. "I think we'd like to hear them now."

I had anticipated this might happen. "Okay," I say, "how about a compromise? We discover what you know first, then I'll hand out a list of nine things other children and their parents have taught me. We can see if the two lists match. Deal or no deal?" Thankfully, Katherine and the rest of the group nod and I quickly begin to write on the flip chart at the front: What we already know about raising great kids!

"Not too much," Tina shouts. She's laughing a little while squirming on her chair. She looks like she's in an exam hall and has suddenly realized she forgot to study.

"I'm sure that's not the case." I ask them each to take a pen and piece of paper from the table beside our circle of chairs and think back to when they were a child. "What did you learn from your parents, or your friends' parents, about raising kids?"

Tina, still anxious, says, "I learned lots about what you don't do. But I'm not sure I learned much about what you should do."

"That's as good a place to start as any. Even a bad life lesson can be helpful, as long as we don't repeat the same mistakes our parents made."

Tina looks skeptical. "My mother's bad parenting can help me help Jemell? God knows it didn't do me much good the first time round."

We all laugh. "I don't think you turned out that bad," I say and look at Ricky to see if he wants to add anything. He just sits quietly smiling at his wife. She gives him a playful shove in return.

I explain to everyone they should first think about their own families and what helped them grow up and cope with life. If they felt their parents were awful parents, they should consider what they think their parents should have done differently. That's the kind of wisdom they'll need to raise their own kids. If they're stumped, and many people I work with are,

I ask them to think of someone else's parent, or a parent figure they've seen on television or in a movie. "Think of the best parent you have ever met. What did they give their children that made a difference?"

I wait a few minutes. Ricky has written just one thing on his paper. Merlinda is writing the first chapter of a book, her mad scribbles filling two pages. I ask them to stop and tell me at least one thing I should write on the flip chart. Quickly, they call out

- love
- discipline
- schooling
- clothing
- people to look up to
- self-esteem
- responsibility
- manners
- a "stick-to-it" attitude
- a sense of humour
- healthy food
- reasonable bedtimes and curfews
- bedtime stories
- grandparents
- church (or other place to worship)

"Any others that aren't already on the list?" I ask. Merlinda considers her notes for a moment. "What about fun stuff, like sports and time to just be a little kid? I think Sadie needs to stop trying to grow up so quick."

"That's a good point." I add "sports" and "fun" to the list. "Any others?"

No one else speaks, but Merlinda cautiously raises her hand. "An extended family. Not just grandparents. And visits to see them. And lots of chances to celebrate with your family. You know. All the things that make a child feel she belongs at home." Her voice cracks a little and Frank folds his hands in his lap, looking down at Merlinda's feet. He is just as upset as she is but is hiding it. I add to the flip chart "extended family" and "family celebrations."

"That's a great list," I say.

Tina crosses her arms as best she can across her large bosom. "Those are all good ideas, but Jemell won't listen to any of it. We invite him to family dinners and he just runs the other way. What do we do then?"

"Would you agree that these things are important? For every child, even if they refuse them when we offer them what they need?" They all nod. "Okay, then. Two things I can tell you with confidence. First, your kids *want you to help them grow up*. And second, little or big, *they want you in their lives*. I can prove it, too."

I ask them to take another sheet of paper and this time think about one thing, just one thing, they've done well as a parent. It might have been one birthday party they held that was their child's best, or maybe it was holding fast to their rules and insisting their child obey curfew. "Describe in a few words a time when you were really proud of how you parented your child. That's what I want to hear."

A minute later I ask them to share what they've written. Everyone has at least one shining moment. Frank raises his hand to speak.

"Feel free to jump in, Frank. No need to raise your hand. I'm not the only teacher here," I tease.

"Okay, then. I think I handled Sadie really well when she asked about getting a tattoo. She's been on about that for months now. But Merlinda and I are dead set against it. She's way too young. But she keeps at us, well, mostly at her mother. I think she figures if we get worn down, we'll give in. And she's right about that. Except, not this time. I don't think children should have tattoos. It's stupid to think the same little kid who just a couple of years ago was dressing in Disney pajamas is ready to paint herself up. She hates clothing we bought her just months ago that she said she loved. How is she going to decide on something she has to wear for the rest of her life?"

"I hadn't thought about it that way. It's a good point you make," I say.

"Thank you. We both think it's a good argument against a tattoo. But last week, we were driving to the mall and Sadie's at us again, and I very calmly said, 'Enough. This conversation is over until you're sixteen.' I liked that. I didn't just say no and drive her nuts. I left her with a promise to revisit the issue, not that I'm likely to budge one little bit. Still, when she's older, she can ask us about this again. But not until then."

"And what did Sadie do?" Katherine asks.

"That's the strange thing. Sadie shut up about it. It's like she finally got an answer she could live with."

We're all quietly reflective for a moment, then I continue around the circle, each group member telling us about a similar moment of triumph. At the end, I ask if there are any other things they think children need.

"You mean like someone to listen to them?" Katherine asks.

"And someone to act in the child's best interests. Protect them from bad decisions," adds Frank. I add both points to the flip chart.

By the time I begin a second wisdom column, I'm pretty sure I've convinced everyone that they know a lot about parenting. I hope they can also see that their children both need them to succeed and want the structure, expectations, and love they have to offer. No matter how often they get pushed aside, parents still matter.

"Now let me show you the nine things I've learned from young people who are in some way or another just like Sadie, Jemell, and Amanda." I hand out cue cards they can keep in their wallets or pin to a bulletin board at home. "I'll have one of these for you every evening we meet."

Nine Things All Children Need

1. **Structure**
2. **Consequences**
3. **Parent-child connections**
4. **Lots and lots of relationships**
5. **A powerful identity**
6. **A sense of control**
7. **A sense of belonging, spirituality, and life purpose**
8. **Rights and responsibilities**
9. **Safety and support**

(This card, and all the others in the chapters that follow, are available at the back of the book in an easy-to-copy layout so they can be carried with you.)

"I know you might not have thought parents had a responsibility to give their kids these things. But this is what parents and kids have taught me. It's what I've seen work exceptionally well turning problem children into flourishing, problem-free young people."

"You'll explain these, right, and how they can help kids like ours?" asks Katherine.

"For sure. And I'll also show you how we, as parents, can juggle all nine at the same time. You see, one without the other doesn't work. Of course, that can make our roles as parents feel as tricky as a circus act."

"You know," says Tina, "I'm surprised how close our list was to yours and everything you told us about Thabo."

I grin, feeling a lot more secure than I did earlier. "There are only two things on my list that you didn't mention. Rights and responsibilities, or what I call social justice, and maybe belonging, as in feeling a part of one's culture. Helping children connect with their grandparents is often the way children learn about their culture and what it really means to be who they are."

"And social justice? That's something parents give kids?" asks Ricky.

"I know it sounds strange but unless a child feels treated fairly at home, at school, and in his community, he's more likely to develop problems. Of course, that means we have to be our children's advocates, defending their rights."

"But still reminding them of their responsibilities?" says Katherine. "You can't forget responsibilities."

"Exactly. You see, all nine things children need work together, like a puzzle." They look satisfied, at least for now.

"All right, parenting gurus, I think it's time we wrap up." They laugh at my goofy joke. Everyone stretches and gets up from their chairs. Coffee cups are put back in the kitchen just like they'd expect their kids to do. The cue cards are folded into the men's wallets or laid in women's purses.

As people leave, I catch snippets of conversation about parking spots and kids who hopefully are still at home. Merlinda pulls me aside after everyone else has left. I'm guessing Frank has gone ahead to get the car. I'm emptying the coffee pot and rinsing the plates. She takes a dishtowel from the top of the fridge and begins to dry. I notice her eyes are as moist as the dishes. Quietly, she tells me, "Sadie's not been coming home after school. I don't know where she is for hours. I didn't want to say anything during the group because I know answers take time, but I'm confused. You understand? I want to work. I don't want to quit and be home after school just to watch her." She gently dries the mug she's holding, inspecting it for any spot that isn't perfectly clean. She avoids looking at me. I keep washing to make this easier for her.

"When she finally did come home yesterday, I yelled at her. I called her a slut. I know I shouldn't have, but she's always thinking about boys. I think that's where she's been. I'm really afraid she'll wind up sleeping with some creepy guy who she meets on the Internet. I don't want her to get pregnant...."

"I'm not sure that if she doesn't come home right away after school, she's sexually active." I am trying to reassure Merlinda that Sadie is a normal teen asserting her independence. "Or being abused. It's possible, of course, but ..." Merlinda is staring out into space, the mug resting on the counter.

"There's something else. I saw her Facebook page. You should see it. She's part of some group. They're called Bitches and Babies. I don't understand, but it's like they're planning to get pregnant. You have to take a look and tell me what you think."

I promise her I'll look. She wipes at her eyes and then lays the wet dishcloth on the counter. "Thank you." She pulls on her coat and lets herself out.

Damn, I think to myself. Why didn't I just tell her to stop the harangue and start talking to her daughter like a young woman? Jeez, Sadie's almost thirteen, obviously precocious in her development, and thinking about boys. Nothing developmentally off the charts about that. Besides, what's Merlinda doing snooping around her daughter's Facebook page? That's not going to improve her relationship with Sadie once the girl finds out.

I sigh. There's no point rushing through this. Next group, I'll see if we can talk about this all together.

I finish the dishes, lock up, and walk home. I'm back before my own thirteen-year-old has gone to bed. Meg is sitting on the couch watching television. I lean down to give her a hug and she lamely pats me on the back. She's like that these days. If I go toward her, she's shy. But as soon as I sit on the sofa with her, she's tucked in next to me, all chatty. "I've got an assignment due next week in history. We're supposed to look at Mesopotamia. That's where Iraq is today." I nod and let our shoulders touch. "I'm going to partner with Oliver."

I can't help myself. "And who's Oliver?"

"You know, the boy in my class who swims? He's been in my class almost every grade since I was eight years old." I know she's rolling her eyes, even if I can't see her face. There's one big advantage of being a university professor. You're excused for being absent-minded.

"Oliver? Oh yes, the tall, stringy one? Looks like a giraffe. Sort of geeky."

Meg ignores my teasing. "He's coming over tomorrow. We're going to work on our Mesopotamia assignment together after school."

There's something in the way she keeps looking at the television and never at me that suggests she wants me to know this but not talk about it. I get the hint and close my mouth. Oliver will be in my home tomorrow with my daughter — my awkward daughter — and I'm not to ask any questions.

After she goes to bed, I go into my office and search the Internet for Bitches and Babies. Google delivers the hit, and a lot of other stuff that leaves my mouth agape. I make a mental note to erase my search history immediately. I sigh. "Girls!" What we have to do as parents to keep them safe!

Boys are easier. My son tells me things. I know where he is, most times. He makes noise. There's nothing subtle about my son. But daughters. It's all innuendo and pouting. I shake my head and exhale a long, troubled breath. It's late and I'm in no mood to think more about Oliver.

Instead, I stare at a sassy-eyed fourteen-year-old on my computer screen who says her name is Jessica. Her hair is cut punk, with spiky, uneven ends. She wears too many earrings to count. She looks like she's starving. "Bitches and Babies is kick-ass feminism," Jessica says. Girls sign on and promise to get pregnant before they're sixteen. Jessica says girls need control over their bodies and that sex is control. She says that girls who have babies are super cool. "The more pregnant you look, the more everyone knows you've had sex. And sex," she tells me, "is f——ing power!" There's more post-feminist ranting. Then instructions. Girls divide themselves by regions. They can meet up if they like. It's like Girl Guides, but for the postpubescent. Each club forms a pact. Sixteen girls agree to get pregnant by the end of their sixteenth year. There is a space on the page for girls to sign up and post a picture. Some show full body profiles, swelling bellies underneath T-shirts. Others show just their faces. Among them is Sadie. She calls herself G(irl)-Spot. I frown and shake my head. Then delete my search history. The last thing I want is Meg finding this crap.

As I turn off the computer, my thoughts turn to Merlinda and Frank. Looks like they do have a problem, and it's not one I'm sure I know how to fix.

Chapter 6

The First Thing Children Need — Structure

"Can you believe it's snowing? It never snows this early." Ricky stomps his feet and shakes the slush from his sneakers. No one was ready for this cold spell. "It's like a Roller Derby out there."

Tina takes her coat off and puts Ricky's arm around her shoulder. "Stand there while I warm up," she tells him. He looks embarrassed but seems to know better than to pull away. We swap that smile guys give each other at times like this. The one that says "I like the attention, but does she have to do this now? Right here?" Tina shows no sign of leaving Ricky's forced embrace anytime soon and Ricky just leans a little forward and does what he's told. How did Jemell ever get to be so much trouble with Ricky as a role model? I have no time to consider an answer. Katherine blows in, shaking snow from her hat. She's early tonight. She doesn't take off her coat even though I've turned the heat up. Merlinda and Frank arrive a couple minutes past seven.

"Good to see you," I tell them. We've already done a quick check-in around the group.

"Damn kid!" Frank says and sits down.

With an opener like that, there's no point in sticking to my agenda. "What happened?" I ask.

"We can be honest here, right?"

"Of course." Everyone is looking at him expectantly.

"So, we've been buying Sadie alcohol when she goes to parties. I know that's dumb, illegal, and all the rest of it. But we figured better she gets a beer or two from us when she's over at her friend's house party than getting some wino to buy it for her and taking all her money. You get into such stupid places with your kids. You know what I mean?"

"I think we all do," I say, trying to reassure Frank that it's okay to have regrets about the decisions we make when it comes to raising kids.

"Now it's not tattoos she wants. Now she's at us about this party coming up on Thursday. That's her birthday and the same day as the school dance. She tells us she's going to go with a bunch of her friends. Then she says, they do drugs, and when my mouth drops, she goes, like, 'So what? You did them, too.' And she's right, of course. She's heard Merlinda and me joke about it. But I wasn't friggin' doing them at thirteen. And then the kicker is she asks us to buy her the drugs! Says, 'You already buy me booze, so why not some pot?' And you know, I didn't know what to say to her. To be honest, I'm glad she's telling me what she's up to, talking to us and all, but drugs? For God's sake! If I don't buy them, assuming my brother who she knows is a bit of a pothead can connect me to his dealer, then what is she going to do? Buy some crap on the street corner or trust some kid to buy it for her? And then who's responsible for her getting into trouble? Having a bad trip. Me and her mother. We'll be the ones she blames." He takes a few moments to catch his breath. Merlinda looks like she wants to retch or crawl under her seat. I'm not sure which would make her feel better. All she does, though, is look at her husband and say nothing.

"Where's that one in the parenting manual?" Frank jokes.

It isn't. Nor is it ever likely to be. But the solution isn't to make matters worse and buy Sadie the drugs. At some point, Sadie needs to know there are limits and consequences to her behaviour.

Frank calms down now that he's shared the impossible situation he's gotten himself into. Ricky reaches over and, to my surprise, pats him on the shoulder. Merlinda and Tina exchange sympathetic looks. I won't say that what Frank did hasn't crossed my own mind, too. But how do we teach them to respect the law once we've helped them to break it?

"Frank," I say after a moment of reflection, "I don't have a short answer for you, but I think what you're asking has a lot to do with tonight's topic: structure." I announce the word as if I'm presenting a platter of succulent roast at a banquet. They don't seem impressed, though they will be. Of all the important things families have taught me over the years, structure — and next week's topic, consequences — stand out as the most critical to a child's safe development. Before I say more about each, however, I begin where I always do, with a story.

Patti was sixteen when I met her. Someone should have begun working with the girl a decade earlier, but instead, she'd been given a hodgepodge of assessments but little by way of treatment. It wasn't that people hadn't tried, but Patti had always been a reluctant child and would quickly burn out everyone who thought they could help — her parents included. By the time I got the referral, she'd been diagnosed with an alphabet soup of labels. ADHD (attention deficit hyperactivity disorder), ODD (oppositional defiant disorder), and CD (conduct disorder) were scribbled across her file, along with terms like borderline personality disorder (a question mark followed that one) and depression. She was described as suicidal, disruptive, truant, and violent.

Funny thing was that Patti wasn't doing all that badly considering the challenges she'd grown up with. Her mother abandoned her when she was six, leaving her with a physically abusive father and spiteful stepmother that Patti referred to only as "the bitch."

I met Patti on the psychiatric ward of a local children's hospital. She'd gnawed at her wrists, ripping veins with her teeth. When she was admitted, her hair was a mess of bloody strands. She hadn't showered in weeks. It took some time to sedate her and get her interested in talking about her life. Mostly Patti just screamed profanities at the nursing staff. She hated being told what to do.

It broke my heart to see her behaving like an obstinate toddler, eyes dark and downcast, refusing to let herself be pulled from her room to play games with the other residents. When I went to visit her and asked her what she thought about her life on the unit, the scars on her wrists, the time spent with her psychiatrist, and meetings with me, she smirked. "None of it's helping. I still feel like shit." Then she curled her feet up under her on the bed and scratched at the bandages on her arm. "Just get my shrink to give me my meds and get me out of here," she said and then went completely mute.

I'm not one to force my clients to do much of anything if they don't want to, but Patti wasn't going to get better until she began fulfilling some promises she'd made to herself and to others. To my mind, we'd given Patti all the excuses she needed to keep her life on hold. With all those labels, no one expected much of the girl, especially Patti herself. When she went completely crazy and began abusing drugs or running away, her family shook their heads and cried but felt powerless to do anything to stop her. "That's Patti," they'd say. "We can't change her so just let her do what she's got to do."

Looking straight at Frank, I tell the group, "I believed that Patti was capable of making better decisions. She just needed us to help her."

I knew she wanted our help when one day, five weeks into her stay, I asked her, "Are there any staff you like at all?" She grunted, which I took to mean yes.

After a brief silence, Patti told me, "A few of them treat me differently from the other girls if I'm not up to doing something. But others, the ones I can't talk to, are always, like, this is the rule. You have to do this! But some staff, they don't break the rules but they bend them, or overlook a rule for a while."

"So you like them to be flexible?" I asked.

"Yeah," she told me. "But not too flexible. It drives me crazy if one night bedtime is nine thirty, the next it's ten thirty. It's supposed to be ten thirty every night. That kind of stuff just messes with my head." I was pleasantly surprised. This crazy girl with the bandaged arms and defiant spirit was telling me she wanted structure. That in the battle of wills, she wanted to know that she was pushing against a wall that most days wouldn't budge. And that for once, someone would give her a sense of predictable security, while still understanding that she was an individual with individual needs.

Frank and Merlinda are listening very closely to what I'm saying.

"Every kid I've ever worked with has told me some variation of this same truth. They all want some rules. Oh, they'll break them, for sure. But they want rules and expectations that the rules are followed."

"So you're saying we shouldn't be buying our daughter dope?" Merlinda asks. She looks quickly at Frank.

"I'm saying that what Sadie may have wanted was a conversation with you about dope, but she didn't necessarily expect you to buy it for her. Likely, what she needed most was for you to say no, but to show you care enough about her to talk with her about the risks involved. Rules alone don't let a child know she's loved. We show compassion for a child when we are also willing to be flexible in how we enforce the rules. If you had yelled at Sadie, or grounded her because there was a risk she would do drugs, I think you would have made her more defiant, and made it even more likely she'll make bad decisions the next time she's with her friends."

"You mean we don't have to agree. We just have to hear her out?"

"Yes. She wants to look into your eyes and know she's on your radar. She's bright enough to know it's not reasonable to ask you to buy her drugs. But she wants to know she's important enough for you to spend the time talking about it with her."

They don't look convinced. "Aren't we, as parents, supposed to set the rules? No ifs, ands, or buts!" Tina says, opening her arms wide enough to embrace the group. It's a gesture that reminds me of a preacher speaking for her congregation.

"Let me answer that with what I've learned from the research on delinquents." I explain that there's a lot of debate about boot camps and whether they are successful getting kids to behave. Boot camps are residential camps for kids with problems that provide a military-like atmosphere involving lots of physical work, exercise, drills, and rules that must be followed. The idea is that the routine and discipline give kids what they need to make better choices in life. We've been treating children in places like this for centuries. Charles Dickens wrote about the workhouses of Victorian England in novels like *David Copperfield* and how such places existed to turn miscreants into good boys and girls. Of course, it didn't work. Harsh living conditions, emotional neglect, and physical punishment do nothing to prepare children for life after the dormitory doors close behind them and they're back in the real world. Alcoholism and lives full of violence are the most common outcomes.

It's the same with boot camps. There's not a shred of evidence that these places help kids. In fact, a careful evaluation of results from forty camps found that only half of them produced any enduring change in children months after discharge.

"Wait, I thought you said boot camps don't change kids," says Frank. "Half of them did."

"That's a really good point. All forty camps provided regimentation and lots of rules, but only half succeeded at their job. Why? The fact is that all that marching and yelling and making beds doesn't really do anything for kids. At least, not alone. The difference between the boot camps that work and the boot camps that don't is whether children receive counselling while at the camp."

"Counselling?" Tina doesn't sound convinced.

I ask her to think back to Patti. A hospital ward is as regimented as a military base. But it heals kids because caring adults are there to listen and make their young patients feel important. Boot camps only work when they do the same. Structure needs connections if it is to help kids grow up well.

"Sadie," I tell Merlinda and Frank, "likely wants the reassurance that you care enough to tell her no, and the sense of security that comes from knowing she can count on someone older than her to help her deal with big decisions. As my friend Barbara Coloroso — a true parenting guru — likes to say, good parenting is like a healthy backbone. It provides children with both structure and flexibility."

Katherine raises her hand. "I get what you're saying. But I'm a single parent. I can't always give Amanda much structure. Sometimes she's got to be responsible for herself. You understand? I can't be there to supervise her. I have to work."

It's a perfect lead into the final thing we need to discuss about structure. The structures we provide must fit with where we live, who we are, and the demands upon us. I can't tell these three families what's right and wrong for their children.

"These things have to be negotiated," I explain. "Some structure is a good thing, but as a family, you're going to have make decisions that suit you and your child. Katherine, I believe that you know best what you and Amanda need."

Katherine has her head cradled in her hands. She's staring at me. "You mean, all those books about when to put your kids to bed, and when they should do whatever, none of that stuff is any good?"

"Those books have some good suggestions, but even the goddess of newborn parenting Penelope Leach makes it clear that parents need to throw away the how-to manual and listen to their baby. You want to breastfeed your child until he has teeth and attends junior kindergarten? A-okay, as long as the child knows how to behave in public and isn't a selfish brat. What I mean is there are lots of things we do as families that are entirely up to us. Like mealtimes, whether beds are made every morning, and how many hours of screen time we allow a child. Those rules will be different for every family.

"Other things aren't so negotiable, no matter what your culture is or which community you live in. Children can't hit other children or adults. They have to go to school. And they should suffer the consequences for their mistakes. We'll talk about consequences next week."

"But Michael, how much structure is enough?" asks Ricky.

"The short answer is, just enough to keep Jemell safe, and no more. That's what the research shows. When researchers interviewed five hundred parents living in poverty in Philadelphia, they found that the parents who had the most rules raised the best kids. Those, of course, were families living within earshot of gunfire on their streets, who could see from their windows the drug dealers and prostitutes that populated their neighbourhoods. Insisting their children go to school and come home right away after school, and tolerating little if any negotiation of house rules, kept kids safe. The children likely knew it, too. That's the right amount of structure for that particular context.

"Now imagine the same rules for a child living in a leafy Atlanta suburb with pleasant parks and a strong municipal tax base that ensures there are enough police available to catch kids drinking beer every time they try to get away with it. The research shows that those kids are going to do well if they are given the freedom to make decisions, within limits, for themselves. No need for the overbearing parent here. Ironically, in upper-middle-class communities, the real danger lurks inside the children's homes, not on the streets outside. The biggest threat to a child's development is a lack of attachment to her parents."

I pull from the closet a television and DVD player and show the first twenty minutes of a documentary titled *The Lost Children of Rockdale County*. The documentary tells the shocking story of youth in a wealthy community on the outskirts of Atlanta that experienced an outbreak of syphilis. More than two hundred young people became infected. These were teenagers who lived in homes with granite countertops and palatial foyers. It's a place where sixteen-year-olds get cars as birthday presents and every child expects to have a television, gaming system, and MacBook to himself.

The homes, though, look sterile. The camera pans across white carpets and Martha Stewart–living rooms so clean and uncluttered one wonders if anyone ever uses them, and if they do, if they ever dare place a drink down on the glass coffee tables.

The real action is up in the kids' bedrooms, where they are invisible to their parents. The youth tell stories of easy access to online pornography and sex parties in which condoms are optional. No surprise there. The parents of Rockdale County were so out of touch with their kids that they thought the pledges the kids had made at church to remain virgins until they married were sincere. The filmmaker's camera shifts its lens from kids talking about group sex to an image of a wall at a local health clinic, where a map shows a tangled web of boys' and girls' names. Each connecting line identifies these young people's multiple sexual partners.

Materially, the kids of Rockdale County had plenty. But their parents, it seems, had abdicated their responsibilities to monitor their children and provide them with the security of their love.

The film has a sobering effect on the group. Merlinda looks like she wants to bolt from her chair and get home as quickly as she can. "So how do we prevent this from happening?" she asks, pleading with me for answers.

"You need to monitor your children enough to keep them safe, but not so much that they can't grow up and learn to be responsible for themselves. Every family and community is different. But all kids, everywhere, want some structure."

Even those Rockdale youth didn't say they were happy doing what they did. They were bored, scared, lonely, and aimless. If it hadn't been sex, it would have been drugs or reckless driving or online poker. The problem isn't the behaviour itself. It's what motivates our children to take stupid risks. I would argue that those Rockdale youth experimented with sex because that was the most frowned-upon activity in a community where most families attended fundamentalist churches. Sex was the most evil thing they could do to express their feelings of abandonment.

Those kids needed much more than Bible readings. They needed the structure that comes with knowing someone is keeping tabs on them and cares enough to sometimes say no, but who will just as often say yes, let me help you. Instead, the children of Rockdale County were given unlimited freedom and no responsibility. Their parents substituted cash for concern. The kids cushioned their feelings of neglect with a trip to the mall. No wonder they treated themselves like prostitutes, their bodies goods to be swapped, poked, and bartered.

Structure, I explain, is reasonable limits, like a bedtime that tells our child when it's time to quiet down and go to her room. It doesn't, however, mean the child has to go to sleep. Structure is what we adults can reasonably control in our children's lives. There are lots of things we want to leave children to do for themselves and suffer the consequences of their decisions. Structure is like a box that we put a child into. It can be quite small when they're two, and much larger when they're twelve. Our job is to ensure that the sides of the box hold fast even while the child launches herself against our rules. But inside the box, that's the child's play zone.

A twelve-year-old, for example, may have a time when she has to go to her bedroom and turn off all her screens (iPod, game console, television, cellphone), but that doesn't mean she has to go to sleep. Want to stay up all night reading? I say, "Go for it, kid, but I'm still going to wake you in the morning and insist you go to school, drowsy or otherwise."

"So how big should the box, I mean structure, be?" asks Katherine.

I invite the group to first consider how old their children are, physically, mentally, and emotionally. "What decisions are your children ready to handle? As long as you are providing responsibilities they can handle and opportunities to fail just *a little,* you are probably providing the right amount of structure. Katherine, I'm going to guess that Amanda wants to choose what she wears when she goes to school. Am I right?" Katherine nods, exaggerating a look of complete defeat.

I smile. "All right. But if she's cold or warm or teased, that's probably good feedback for her about the decisions she's been given to make. She'll get better at making good decisions the more she's allowed to practise with decisions that have consequences she can handle herself." I pause for a moment to let everyone think about that.

"Now, second, ask yourself, what is normal in my family? At my child's school? In my community?" I never listen to a child who tells me "All the other kids ..." and then makes outlandish claims of incredible privilege. "Trust me on this. As a family therapist, I don't meet well-functioning families with children who stay up really late on school nights, or never have to clean their room, or get eight hours of screen time a day. There are children like that, but we usually call them neglected." The parents look reassured hearing that they can say no.

"As a family you can, and should, make decisions that reflect your culture and values. A child who is treated respectfully and within the range of normal will usually, eventually, agree to the rules you set. A five o'clock curfew on a weeknight for a fourteen-year-old is excessively strict. But what about 9:00 p.m.? 10:00 p.m.? Midnight? Deciding what the right rule is will always be a matter of negotiation. But the rules should make you feel comfortable, too — at least up to a point. If you are too comfortable, your child may be safe, but will he have the opportunities he needs to grow? And that means suffering the consequences when he makes bad decisions."

I explain that we, as parents, need to ask ourselves "What is appropriate in my culture? And in my community?" For example, it's not unusual for families from different religious backgrounds to insist on appropriate clothing for children or to prefer their daughters (and sometimes their sons!) to abstain from dating until they are older than many of their peers who are allowed to date. Does this rule make the child stand out? Will she rebel? The likely answer to both questions is yes. But will it hurt the child or lead to problem behaviour? Likely not. A child who sees these rules as part of her parents' culture, and is being invited to participate in that culture, will at least know that her parents are trying to be reasonable. A young woman may disagree but she's unlikely to think her parents are intentionally trying to make her life difficult.

I turn to the flip chart and write:

Ways Parents Can Provide Their Children with the Right Amount of Structure

Then I give one suggestion to get us started.

- Give young people second chances when they break rules or make mistakes.

Everyone is fine with that and we brainstorm other strategies we've used. In a few minutes, we have a pretty good list of possible ways families can provide children with structure.

- Give children chores that make a contribution to the well-being of others in the family (that includes their siblings, parents, and even family pets).
- Expect children to behave when they are out in public.
- Expect children to attend school and do their homework.
- Know where children are at all times, but give them permission to roam their neighbourhood on their own.
- Provide children with their own cellphones and ask them to pay a portion of the monthly bill.
- Teach children how to negotiate rules respectfully at home and at school. Coach them on how to disagree with adults (even their parents) without becoming rude.
- Share stories with your children about your life as a child and the structure (or lack of structure) you had growing up. Ask them if what you experienced is good or bad for children today.
- If you are raising children as a couple (or with other adults like grandparents and babysitters), be sure the adults all agree on what structure children should expect.
- As children grow up, be sure to change the rules to match children's capacity to solve their own problems.

I promise to email the list to them the next day. "Maybe I'll show Jemell the list," says Tina. "Let him choose his poison!" We all laugh.

I notice the time. "Let me review what we've talked about tonight." As everyone stretches, I pass around a printed wallet-size card as a reminder.

Things Our Children Need
1. Structure

- Children want a reasonable amount of structure. It convinces them that their parents love them.
- The structure parents provide children needs to make sense to the children themselves. It needs to fit with where children live, the dangers they experience, and the values that their families hold.
- Children are okay with being told no when what they want puts them in real danger.
- As often as possible, children need to hear yes and be encouraged to take responsibility for themselves and others.

As the parents gather their coats, I lean over to Merlinda and Frank and ask them if they need to talk more about Sadie.

"I looked at that Facebook page." ·

Merlinda looks at Frank, her shoulders slumping forward. "Maybe we can stay for a minute?"

After the others have left, I pour myself a cup of tea and refill Merlinda and Frank's cups with what remains of the coffee. It looks like molasses but they gladly accept it, perhaps hoping for a wake-up jolt that will bring with it a solution to Sadie's problems.

"Do you have any thoughts about why Sadie is trying to get pregnant? Why this makes sense to her?"

Merlinda bites her bottom lip. "I don't know, but I think she might already be sexually active. With one of the boys in the next grade. I went to check her homework in her binder. It was just inside her school bag. And I had to empty her lunch bag, too." I can't imagine Sadie left her bag for her mother to snoop in by accident. I'm wondering what she's really up to. "I found some poetry on the back cover of her binder. It was ..." Merlinda begins to cry.

"It was about a boy and, well, about sex. With him," says Frank. "This is getting so out of hand."

I can't help but feel Sadie is telling us something. Something she wants us to know but can't, or won't, come right out and say. "It sounds like it's time for us all to meet again." They both agree and I schedule a meeting for early the next week before the group gets back together.

"You know, I think the other parents might be willing to support you on this. If you want to talk to them about it, too."

"Yes," says Merlinda, "I think I know that. I think Tina is feeling the same about Jemell. Only he's a boy, of course."

"It's totally up to you," I say, and gently say goodnight.

Chapter 7

The Second Thing Children Need — Consequences

If my father didn't take very good care of me, I can only imagine the care he received from his own mother and father. I have not one story, good or bad, to tell my children about their great-grandparents. My father never spoke about them. Not even once.

They were both dead by the time I was two. All I know about my grandfather's past is that he went to work in the textile factories in Montreal's north end when he was still just a boy, sweeping factory floors and studying night courses at college when he was older.

My aunt Esther, my father's eldest sister, was the only relative I ever met from his side of the family. When I was twelve and pushing for details about my grandparents, she told me that her father emigrated from Hungary in 1902 when he was still a child. That's all she'd tell me before getting up and busying herself in the kitchen. The rest of my father's family, even his brothers and sisters, is a mystery. I don't even know how many siblings there are.

Only Aunt Esther ever graced our dinner table. It's not much to build a story from, but if I look carefully, there are puzzle pieces that snap together. Aunt Esther sent me birthday cards with five-dollar bills stuffed inside. And there were visits to her apartment, where she lived with my uncle Abe.

I liked those outings. My father could always be convinced to drive extra fast over the steep little railway bridge on the way to see her. If I was lucky enough to be sitting way in the back of the station wagon, and he went very fast over the hump, I'd feel weightless and woozy, just like on a roller coaster. At least one of those visits was always early in May when the weather was milder and we could walk in sneakers rather than winter boots. If I remember correctly, most were on Mother's Day.

My father wouldn't be the first child to have had an older sister who is, in truth, his mother. But I'm still left to guess who my grandfather really is. I have a feeling in my gut that Uncle Abe wondered as well why this younger brother was so special to his wife. Or why my aunt Esther was so reluctant to talk about her father.

"I think your mom and dad are really worried about you getting pregnant."

"Like that's any of their business." Sadie sits in my office, arms crossed. Merlinda is next to her on a red office chair.

Frank chose not to attend. He sounded uncomfortable when he phoned to apologize. "Something's come up," he told me. I didn't push, knowing that we would be talking about his stepdaughter's sex life.

Merlinda grips the arms of her chair tightly and I see her mouthing words that don't get said. I want to tell her, "Please, say what you need to say" but instead hold my tongue, afraid Sadie will think we have a pact against her.

Instead I ask Sadie, "Can you explain to your mom how this makes sense?" I want to give Sadie the right to make decisions for herself, even if she has only just turned thirteen.

Sadie rolls her eyes, takes a deep breath, as if she's entirely bored with me already. But she isn't, really. She wants to tell me her side of the story. I'm not accusing her of doing anything wrong. As long as I don't do that, I think she'll talk to me.

"It's a girl-liberation thing. We studied in school *Lysistrata*. You know, that play by some old Greek guy." Merlinda looks a little lost. I explain about Aristophanes and his story about the women of ancient Athens and Sparta, who are tired of their men always starting wars. The women tell the men that until they stop the Peloponnesian War, they will not be welcome in the beds of their wives and lovers.

"Only we think we're more powerful if we have sex. On our terms." Merlinda looks pale and I excuse myself for a moment to get her a glass of water. As Merlinda drinks, Sadie continues talking. "So we have a club, of sorts. Just a Facebook page. Girls decide who to do it with, and if you conceive a baby, then jackpot. You're supposed to get pregnant by sixteen."

Merlinda doesn't look any less confused even with the explanation. "You mean, honey, you want to have a baby? This is some sort of feminist thing?"

"Yeah, why not?" Sadie slides slowly down in her seat, her spindly legs straight out, boots crossed. "You may have screwed things up with Dad, and made me a mess, but that doesn't mean I can't raise a kid better than you did. I don't mean the guy has to marry me or anything like that. Yech! I just want him to know that I decided to have our baby, and he and I are connected forever."

"That doesn't make any sense. He'll just leave you."

"No, he won't. I won't let him. You know, grrrl power and all that." Sadie growls and crimps her hands in front of herself like claws.

"But you don't know the first thing about babies. I still remember when you came home and told me Marla Popowicz told you babies came out your bum, and you thought she was so much smarter than all the other girls that you believed her. And I had to tell you the truth."

Sadie is ignoring her mother by staring at my bookshelf. The more her mother speaks, though, the more she flushes red and clenches her jaw. "I was right then, wasn't I?" Merlinda continues. "I'm right now, too, when I tell you, Sadie, you don't want a baby."

Sadie finally rolls onto one hip and points a finger accusingly at her mother. "Oh, you mean you never wanted me, then?"

Was that the question that was waiting to be asked? Merlinda is shocked by what Sadie has just said. Hesitantly, she looks at me, then back toward her daughter.

"Of course," she says in a voice heavy with the tears that are welling up inside, "I wanted you." Her voice is pleading with her daughter to believe her. "Your real father thought he did, but then he changed his mind. He got scared. But Frank loves you as much as any father can love his daughter. Sadie, he really does." Merlinda is crying now, but Sadie is doing nothing to make this easier for her. "I was so happy to have you, even though your father left us. I still wanted you. But I was only seventeen and it wasn't easy. You've got to know, I was so young."

Sadie jumps up from her chair, knocking it backwards. "Screw you. My father was messing around with lots of women before he died. Right? You don't like to say it, but you weren't enough, and I wasn't enough, to keep him. He hated us. Why don't you tell the truth? He hated you! He hated me, too." She is standing with her hands over her face, trying to keep in the loud sobs that are being pulled from her. She tries to suck them back in but can't. Merlinda doesn't stand up but lays a hand on Sadie's elbow. Sadie shakes her away and moves toward my door.

"Sadie, please, come back and sit with your mom. She's heard you. Let's see what she can tell you."

"No!" she yells and runs from the room.

Merlinda stays where she is. She's flustered. Tiny beads of perspiration appear on her upper lip. Her eyes are now vacant black marbles set amid the wrinkled tanned skin of someone who is fighting to rewrite her own girlhood. Merlinda must have been a beautiful young woman when she was seventeen and the stress of life was still a distance into the future. She still exudes a subtle sexuality that must confuse a daughter who is the poster child for the emaciated prepubescent punk rocker: slight, shoulders drooped, with twig-thin arms. Her mother was fuller a moment ago. Now she, too, looks like Sadie — ashen and gaunt.

I look at Merlinda. "At least we now know what this is about."

"I'm not sure I understand."

"What Sadie said. About having a baby as a way of putting her back in control of men like her father. Of her life. Maybe of showing you up. Of doing better than she thinks you did. Or maybe of healing the wound caused by losing her father."

"It's been so many years. I never knew she thought about him like that."

"Maybe it's the same for all those girls. Sex, boys, babies — these are things they can do themselves whether their parents agree or not. We adults think abstinence and holding back are power. But for some girls — those girls — getting pregnant is power."

"Yes, but a baby, if it comes, will be my problem."

"I know that." We both sit quietly for a few moments gathering our thoughts. Then Merlinda takes out a makeup kit and touches up her lipstick and eyeliner. I wait.

"Thank you," she says as she gets out of her chair quickly and walks, head high, lips still quivering, from my office.

The next evening, the group has barely sat down before Tina speaks. "Jemell's not talking to me. He says I embarrass him. Like, what? I don't have a right to talk anymore?" Everyone looks a little confused, myself included. Tina sits up straight, hands folded in her lap. She has been waiting days to share her story.

"What happened?" I ask, grinning at her enthusiasm.

"Well, all I did was tell my son and the other boys who were in my car that I didn't like their music." Ricky gives her a stern look. I'm sure he, too, wishes she hadn't said anything to their son and his friends.

"What?" Tina says, staring right back at him, then continuing to tell her story undeterred.

"They were listening to some glam rock band that's been around for years and years. For God's sake, their music was crap when I was growing up and still is! All dressed up in satin suits so tight you can see everything, if you know what I mean. So I said to the boys that they made me think of a bunch of old men in spandex doing yoga, showing off their tea bags." Everyone, even Ricky, is laughing.

"I thought they'd appreciate my humour," Tina says. "But no. Jemell was so mad he slammed the car door when I let him out at the mall and now he won't talk to me. Honestly, you'd think he thinks we found him in a basket by the river. All *they* do is talk about sex. How could *I* have embarrassed *him*?"

Frank slaps his thighs. "Kids, they're all the same."

"God forbid if we have sex lives," Tina says, mocking her son. It's good to see everyone, even Merlinda, laughing and jelling as a group.

"I guess our kids don't really want us to be their friends, do they?" I say as the laughter subsides. Everyone nods.

"But they say they do," says Ricky. "They want to tell us all about what they're thinking, but we're not supposed to judge or do anything to help them. No rules, nothing. You talk about structure, sure, but that's not what they say they want, now is it?"

"Good point. But just because they hate us sometimes, that doesn't mean they don't want us to act like parents and enforce some rules. Last meeting we talked about structure and expectations. Tonight I want to explore consequences. If you take anything from tonight, then hear me when I tell you that the families I've worked with over the years say you've got to get this right. Structure is like your right hand; consequences, your left. Clasp them together and you have a nice firm embrace around your kid." On the flip chart I draw a picture of two clasped hands, both with wristbands. On one wristband I write "structure" and on the other, "consequences."

So why didn't Jemell appreciate Tina's joke? Likely because Jemell doesn't want a mother who is his friend. The word counsellors use is *boundaries*. Parents and children need appropriate boundaries. Oh sure, there are lots of times boundaries can be renegotiated and changed, but kids are reassured when they know where the limits are. They also need to know what to expect when they break the rules. Give them structure and consequences, and they are far less likely to become problem children.

A story may help to make the point, but before I can begin, Katherine interrupts. "Michael, rather than you telling the story tonight, can I?" And so it's my turn to sit back in my chair and listen.

"My daughter Amanda is still too young to know things about me, but I didn't learn very much about being a good parent from my folks. Every time they enforced the rules, I ran away. First, when I was just a child like Amanda, I ran to my friends, then later to a shelter for homeless youth. But I wasn't homeless — just a bratty young woman who didn't want to do anything I was told. So my parents did something they weren't very proud of. In the middle of the night, they changed the locks. They had to do something. They sort of knew that, well … this is really hard for me to say, but I was selling myself. Not for money, but sleeping with any old pervert to get drugs and a place to sleep."

"I'd kill the creep I caught doing that to Sadie," Frank says.

Katherine ignores him, perhaps afraid to admit she wishes her own father had been better at protecting her from herself. "Mind you, my parents made sure I had a place to go. They left me a note on the door: 'You can go to Chelsea's house if there is a bed available.' Chelsea was my best friend. Of course, I didn't go to Chelsea's." Katherine begins to cry. "It was so horrible, there on the street late at night, all alone. But what else could they do? I was still fifteen and I wouldn't listen to anyone!"

"Katherine, were there problems like this before you got to be an adolescent?" I ask.

"I was just turning eleven when we moved, and my older brother died. From a drug overdose. My God, I hated when my mother would say that I was acting up because I was sad about my brother dying. I'd insist his death had nothing to do with anything. I didn't want to hear anything bad about him, either. Or remember that my parents were always fighting with him. I think I blamed them for not looking after him better. Now I can see my brother was an asshole. He treated my parents really badly. He practically ignored me, too. Missed all my birthdays. Was always high. But after he died, I forgot all that stuff. I guess I was afraid that I was going to end up just like him."

"You've done just fine, honey," says Tina as she places a hand on Katherine's shoulder and leans toward her. "Boys at that age can be so selfish. They don't think who they're hurting. They'll throw their lives away."

Wiping away her tears, Katherine continues to tell her story. "I guess a lot of what's wrong with Amanda is my fault." Tina tries to disagree but Katherine will have none of her sympathy. "I never expected her to get good grades. I just wanted her to pass and enjoy her school years, her childhood. I didn't want to give her medications. I wanted to believe that she was normal. Because I never was. I couldn't accept that Amanda is headed for the same life I've lived." She pauses to catch her breath and knot her hands together. "I'm so worried about what will happen when she reaches puberty. That's when I lost interest in school. Me and my friends, we'd wander around, cutting class. I always smelled of cigarettes or pot when I came home. And even now, the kids Amanda hangs out with after school, when I'm not home to supervise her, they smell like that, too. It's driving me crazy. You know we live in one of the housing projects? I can't afford a place that isn't subsidized. But I don't want Amanda to grow up among a bunch of problem kids who remind me of myself at that age.

Michael, you talk about structure. Try giving that to a kid when all around you there's nothing but families with problems."

Katherine is quiet for a moment, gathering her thoughts. She blows her nose with a tissue she pulls from the box I hand her.

"The real problem, I think, is that Amanda doesn't appreciate anything I've done for her. I work hard, try to make her life easy. And all I ask is that she go to school, and ..." Katherine's voice breaks, "not run away from me. Oh, I'm such an awful parent."

I lean forward in my chair and catch Katherine's eye. She looks so deflated, her black eyeliner streaking her cheeks. "Thank you, Katherine, for the story. Let's see what we can learn from what you've just shared with us." I gently change the focus from Katherine and her daughter Amanda to what we know about consequences.

Whether their children are six or sixteen, parents need to insist they are held accountable when they let others down. Amanda needs Katherine to enforce some rules. She also needs to understand there are consequences if she doesn't come home after school and doesn't do her homework. A year-old child, as surely as a nine-year-old or a fifteen-year-old, needs to understand that if you put yourself in danger, you are going to suffer consequences.

I've learned a lot about consequences from families like the three I'm looking at. Mostly, I've been shown there's a difference between consequences that punish and those that offer discipline. I ask the parents to think about adopting a dog from the SPCA that has been abused and behaves badly. An irresponsible owner punishes a dog to try to scare it into submission. But we know that a dog with a history of being beaten, or one that has been chained outside for weeks in the sun, its skin growing over its collar, its emaciated body dehydrated, and its temperament wild and unpredictable, could never be turned into a well-behaved, well-disciplined household pet by being beaten some more.

So how did we ever come to believe that if we "spare the rod, [we] spoil the child"? As hard as it might be to believe, the truth is that the number of delinquent children is *decreasing* in most industrialized nations because we have stopped the antiquated abuse of our children that we once called discipline. Both boys and girls are less likely today to get into trouble with the law. There are a lot of reasons for this change, not the least of which is that we are getting better at teaching children to tell us what they need. And we're showing them how to resolve conflict without beating one another with a stick, rod, belt, spoon, or their hands.

There is not one single piece of research anywhere that shows hitting a child is an effective parenting strategy. "Don't let anyone convince you otherwise," I tell the group. "No serious psychologist, social worker, or member of any religious order has shown that corporal punishment prevents or corrects children's bad behaviour better than showing that child empathy and teaching him how to solve problems without violence."

I pause and let my words land hard. "Let's think about what children like Amanda, Jemell, and Sadie really need," I say, looking at each parent as I say their child's name. "Here are a few questions to ask yourselves if you want to raise children who will become kind, loving adults capable of raising their own children." I go to the flip chart and begin writing as I speak.

"Does your child know you are monitoring her behaviour? Children need secure and predictable places in which to grow. They need to be absolutely certain someone cares enough about them to provide them with an environment where their impulses to hurt others or themselves will be controlled and consequences guaranteed. It's a scary world for children who push at the boundaries of being horrible people but are never told, 'That is not acceptable. You must stop.'

"Does your child know what will happen if she is abusive toward you, her siblings, or anyone else?

"Does she know the consequence for being irresponsible or for not doing what is reasonably expected of her? I want my child to learn that if she makes mistakes, things will happen that she'll have the responsibility to make right again. That's what I call natural consequences. Do something bad, and your mistake causes a problem for you, not someone else. A good consequence is one that motivates a child to fix her own problem because its too uncomfortable not to fix it."

I stop talking for a moment, realizing I know in every fibre of my being how important good consequences are. My thoughts drift back to my childhood and the basement workshop where I spent much of my time when I was nine years old. I had pleaded with my father to teach me how to use his hand tools, then his power tools. At first he sensibly refused, arguing I was too young. But I was always sneaking in there, anyway. It got to be so dangerous that he figured it would be better if he just went ahead and showed me. It's the only memory I have of us spending much time together. My mother, thankfully, had no interest in what took place in the shop. My father taught me about chisels, hand drills, and backsaws. I remember him showing me how to push — never pull — the chisel into the wood. I remember him showing me first an electric sander, then an electric drill, and finally a jigsaw. I made birdhouses and doll furniture for my baby sister, whom we'd adopted the year before. Everyone was proud of what I made, but my father — I remember — he beamed.

He wasn't there the day I drove a quarter-inch chisel deep into my left thumb. He was away on business and I was working with a piece of oak I'd found in the bin at the back of the shop. The wood was beautifully grained but much harder than the pine I usually worked. I had clamped the stock into a vise and was trying to shave the corners to make a toy car. Only I couldn't put enough force behind the chisel to get it to cut the wood cleanly. In a moment of forgetfulness, I held the block with my left hand and grabbed the chisel like an ice pick, then pulled it down the side of the block. The first pass shaved the wood nicely, but the second pass against the smoothness of the first came sharply and quickly, stabbing the blade deep into my thumb.

I don't remember crying, but instead being horribly worried that I'd never be allowed back into my father's shop. I'd have done anything to hide what I'd done, but there was nothing I could do except walk upstairs with my hand wrapped in a towel and show my mother the chisel stuck there.

She slapped me.

The memory brings me back into my body. My hand rises to my cheek and I am suddenly aware that I'm speaking.

"So let me ask all of you, how do you create the right amount of structure and the natural consequences that follow for your children?" Hearing my own words, I am again grounded in the room.

"I'm not sure I've been very good at that at all. That's why Amanda hasn't been coming home after school like I tell her to," says Katherine.

Still scrambled from my daydream, I answer, "Let's think about some times in the past when you feel you did give Amanda," I pause and look at the other parents, "and Sadie and Jemell exactly what they needed."

"We give Sadie chores," Frank says.

"And I won't give Amanda any money unless she helps around the house."

I nod with enthusiasm and begin to write down what they say. Occasionally I add lessons I've learned from other families. And I think of what my own father taught me. About how he came home to my mother's complaints about the harm I'd done with the chisel and her insistence that he keep me out of his shop. Reluctantly, I met him in the kitchen and showed him the large flap of skin that dangled open when I removed the gauze bandage. He hissed a little between his teeth and held my hand for a brief moment. Then he frowned and told me to be careful next time. "Always push a chisel." I waited, expecting more. He sat down and began to eat his dinner, while I pondered the beauty of natural consequences.

Our children need the freedom to make choices, mess up, and then suffer what comes next. If a three-year-old hits, he should have some time away from others until he is ready and able to control himself. If he bites, he needs to be taken away from the situation that is frustrating him, then helped to understand what he did and who he hurt.

"Just remember, as parents, we control the size of the box surrounding our child, and the consequences that she suffers when she makes mistakes," I say, trying to sound wise, though knowing very well how difficult this is to put into practice with one's own children.

Letting a four-year-old play quietly with his toys on the floor in his room after lights out means letting him make decisions for himself. But then how to teach him the consequences the next morning when he's a grumpy, rude little boy at the breakfast table? Take away his right to watch television for a day? That seems silly. How is that privilege connected to the bad choice he made the night before? Children will understand and accept natural consequences when they make sense. It's better, I think, to remove his toys from his room, or insist he remain in his bed after his light is turned off. He still doesn't have to go to sleep if he doesn't want to, but he can't play on the floor, either. At least not until he learns to modulate his behaviour himself.

It's not easy, though, to know how much to let children suffer the consequences of their own decisions.

Don't be *nice*. Be *kind* instead.

Give your child the structure she needs in the amount she needs it and let consequences match mistakes. We all know that we can avoid arguments by pandering to our tantrumming child, but we also know that we won't raise a problem-free child if we always give in. We'll eventually be dealing with an adolescent who is calling us names, breaking curfew, stealing liquor, and chronically truant from school.

"So, not enough structure, and our kids will wind up in detox, as messed up as a Hollywood rock star. But too much? What happens then?" I can see Ricky is looking for the recipe book. Unfortunately, it's just not that simple.

Katherine, though, is ready with an answer. "He becomes some boy messing around in my daughter's bed. A boy who doesn't give a damn about who he knocks up or what happens to his kid afterward."

"Ain't that the truth," Tina agrees, playfully poking her husband in the ribs.

"Based on my experience with lots of families, that boy is less likely to be in that bed if he understands there are consequences to what he does," I say. "And Amanda's not likely to grow up and be there, either, if Katherine keeps doing all the good things she's doing." Katherine gets a high-five from Tina, and they both giggle like schoolgirls.

"There are obvious differences between providing punishment and discipline," I explain. "Parents have taught me that discipline is fine to give a child. But remember, threatening a child with unfair rules or using physical punishment, humiliation, or abandonment — none of these strategies are going to prevent you raising a child riddled with problems. Sorry, but that's the truth."

I explain that a child of any age appreciates knowing there are limits and that someone cares enough to enforce them with compassion. That means the child knows before he breaks the rules what is a reasonable consequence. Good discipline starts with well-defined expectations and full disclosure of what is likely to happen if a child decides to go his own way. It ends with the guarantee that what is supposed to happen, happens. Quickly.

"Sounds remarkably simple, doesn't it? Your eight-year-old is hitting his six-year-old sister. You've told him if he hits, he goes to his room until he's calmed down and is able to apologize and mean it. The trouble is, you don't actually see him hitting his sister. You only hear his sister yelling at the top of her lungs, 'Stop that!' and when you enter the room, she's got her fingernails clawing at his arm. What then?"

"'She's hitting me,' your son complains as you tear the little girl, now sobbing violently, from her brother while she yells, 'He was pulling my hair!'

"If your stomach is churning already, you're not alone. You just have two normal kids who need to know what's coming next. Try telling them, 'You two can't play together if you are going to fight. Because I didn't see who started this, to your rooms, both of you.' A little later you may want to set some reasonable expectations. 'If you get hit, come and tell me. If you hit back, expect to be in your room for a while.'"

Ricky and Tina nod vigorously. They've obviously been living episodes like this for years. "Of course, after the forty-third episode of this sibling version of cage wrestling, you might be excused for considering growling like a mother bear at the children or wanting to take a swat at both of them yourself. Growling a little isn't likely to do much harm, but swatting, spanking, or slapping isn't going to change their behaviour over the long term. Physical violence is punishment. A big person beating on a little person is punishment. It teaches children only how to abuse their power to make others do what they want them to do. I'll bet your son already understands well how to punish his sister. It's time the adults in his life taught him something different."

Ricky waves at me to stop. "But what if the child is fifteen, instead of five? And he hits his sister, or worse, swears at his father?"

"Hmm. Good question. Again, I'd think of consequences rather than punishment. My goal is to make my child respect me. I can't see how I do that by hurting him physically or emotionally. I also don't want him to grow up and talk to his spouse or children like he's talking to me at that moment. If I don't do something, and show him through my actions how to behave, I'm handing someone else my problem." Ricky quietly considers what I've just said.

It's easier to help older children anticipate consequences before problem behaviour occurs. What is the house rule about swearing at one another? You can't send a fifteen-year-old to his room. What if he says he won't go? But chances are, that young man relies on you for many things. Rides to see his friends? Money for music lessons? Extra-special, trendy clothing? His favourite food or snack? Not to mention clean laundry. Before you get angry, consider what you are trying to teach him, and let him know what he can expect if he is rude or violent.

"Maybe I can explain this in the same way I do when I'm coaching a family in my clinical practice. Let's take this in three steps. Say, for example, a child swears at his father. First, tell him that swearing at others in the family is disrespectful and makes it difficult to feel good about being together.

"Second, tell him that swearing degrades others, and this is a family where one hopes people will try to make each other feel special. If he wants you to make him feel special, it's his responsibility to makes others feel the same.

"And third, explain that swearing is a form of intimidation. It makes others frightened. This is a family where we all want to feel safe."

A child who refuses to make his home a respectful, supportive, and safe environment doesn't really deserve the advantages of living in a home like that. While we can't abandon the child (that's a form of punishment and makes the child feel less connected, less loved), we can send him a message that his family is there for him if he wants to participate in a way that honours everyone's interdependence. If he doesn't want to participate on those terms, then he can certainly live more independently.

"It's actually quite simple to put into practice," I explain, "even if the words sound complicated."

When he wants a drive, remind him there are buses and taxis. (He can pay for these himself, using his allowance or birthday money if he has any.) If he needs new clothes, there are always items on sale or available very cheaply at the Salvation Army store. There is no need to spend big bucks on name brands to make a child feel happy when that same child can't be bothered to contribute to making others feel good. It's the same for food as well as laundry. We parents do a lot for our children. It is reasonable to expect them to do something in return.

A child who is raised to think of himself as part of an interdependent family is a child who is unlikely to make a mess of his relationships later in life.

"So what do you think?" I pause to let these ideas settle. Tina looks at Ricky and Ricky stares at his feet.

"I don't think we could do that. Jemell would destroy the house if we didn't buy him at least some of what he asked us for. He would be so out of control, I'd worry for our safety," Tina says, exasperated. I take a deep breath and try to hide my own frustration. It's difficult to figure out how great people like these two are getting checkmated by a teenage bully.

"It's difficult to change patterns," I say, and count to three, finding deep inside myself a place where I can stash my self-doubts. Can any of this really change Jemell? Rubbing my hands together, I decide it's best to just repeat what I've heard the kids themselves tell me. "Here are two secrets you need to remember. First, Jemell wants — no, *needs* — you to stand up to him and insist he act more responsibly experience real consequences for his problem behaviour. And second, delaying these life lessons only places your son in *more* danger. If you don't hold him accountable now, then who will? Consider this: If you don't accept a colleague at work yelling at you, then why in God's name would you accept such rudeness in your own home? What's more, why would we want to teach a child that this behaviour is tolerated?

"Try doing this for the next week and tell me how it goes. Figure out what Jemell relies on you to do for him and hold back everything but the necessities until he agrees to participate in the family in a way that adds to its cohesion. If I'm wrong, I'm willing to help you try something different. If I'm right, or better, if the children and families who taught me these rules are right, then let's celebrate your success as a group next week."

"Sounds fair," Ricky says.

"Okay, then. I've told you all about structure and consequences. As good as these two principles sound, you still need one more foundation stone to raise a problem-free child. But it only makes sense once you understand how important structure and consequences both are." They are looking at me like I'm about to share the meaning of life.

"This third piece is the easiest one to put into practice. It's the thing we parents already most want." I pause to make sure they're listening. "We need to stay connected to our child."

"That's all?" asks Merlinda. "Stay connected? That sounds easy."

"I don't know," says Katherine. "It seems like the more structure I give Amanda, and the more consequences I lay on her, the less connected we become."

"It can feel like that. Maybe you'll feel differently after hearing what I have to say. Next week."

There is a collective "Awww" and then they chuckle. "It's like a television series," Tina jokes, while pouting. "I hate cliffhangers."

I promise them we'll talk about connections in lots of detail next week, then pass out another wallet-size card with notes about tonight's discussion.

Things Our Children Need
2. Consequences

- Our children want the security of knowing there are reasonable consequences to their actions.
- Our children want to be shown how to fix their mistakes without using violence or bullying others that are weaker than they are.
- Our children need to be reminded they are part of their families, schools, and communities, and are accountable for the harm they cause others.
- Our children need quick and thoughtful discipline that models empathy, not harsh punishment that teaches them how to hurt others.

Chapter 8

The Third Thing Children Need — Parent-Child Connections

I have a secret to share. I wanted to love my father, but I kept my distance. It was the only way I knew to avoid feeling worthless.

Of course, it wasn't like that when I was younger. Then, I wanted his attention. I liked how he encouraged me to stand up for myself.

I still remember being told to talk back to the librarian in grade three who wouldn't let me read books in the part of the library reserved for the older kids.

"Tell her you have my permission to read those books," is what my father said. I wanted him to tell her. But he ignored me and just kept reading the paper.

The next day, all on my own, I had to look up and into Mrs. Elliot's immense, foreboding face, with its stubbly beard and wart with the three hairs sticking out, and explain to her in my very nicest voice that my father said I could read the grade four books if I wanted to.

I still remember how she had frowned then huffed, "Fine," and left me completely lost among stacks of books that I guess she thought were dangerous. Their battered spines tempted me with titles like *Space Exploration* and *The Decline of Dinosaurs*.

I won that battle, but I never told my father I'd won. I just brought the books home and laid them on the living room table by the television hoping he'd notice. He never did.

• • • •

With Jemell on house arrest, it's not difficult to convince him to come and meet with me and his parents. At the very least, it's time outside his home. I ask Tina and Ricky to let me ask Jemell some questions before I bring them into the conversation. I'm hoping to convince Jemell my office is a safe place where he can tell his own story.

It works magically. Within minutes, Jemell is convinced he won't be interrupted. He tells me about what it was like growing up, a black kid in a white community.

"We were the only black family and it was okay at first, but then because I was this fat little black kid, all the other kids began to bully me, jump me. So I began to fight back. I even took karate classes." It proved a good solution at first, but soon Jemell was in fights all the time. When the other kids began to double up and attack him in pairs, he started bringing knives to school.

"I'm not a great fighter. But the thing you need to know about me is that I won't let myself get beaten. If I have to pull a weapon, I'll pull a weapon."

"Let me see if I understand that," I say. "You're not the greatest fighter, but if you pull a knife, it evens the odds. Any other way you avoid fights?"

"I smoke pot. It calms me down." Jemell looks at Ricky, who is squirming, waiting to speak. "I don't see how they can disagree. My whole family does it. And my dad, he told me as long as I don't bring it around the house he's fine, because he was young once and he knows how it is."

"Wait a minute," interrupts Ricky, unable to hold back any longer. "I never said it was okay...."

"Maybe we can let Jemell say what he needs to say first, then respond?" I jump in, trying to prevent an argument.

"I just meant he shouldn't be doing it around us and his brothers and sisters at home."

"Yeah, whatever," says Jemell, his tone contemptuous. "It's still the only thing working to fix my nerves. Because there are a lot of guys at school giving me trouble. Like this one guy, he's calling me a n——, and I say to him, well then, meet me outside, and he says, 'Sure bitch,' and so I'm waiting for him outside. Me and my buddy B-Top. We're not taking any of this shit. And so when we see him outside, I run up behind him and say, 'You got something to say now?' and he says, 'Oh yeah,' and then he drops his school bag and says, 'Come on, you little bitch,' and I drop my shit and give B-Top all my earrings and chains and do what had to be done."

I lean back in my chair, thinking hard about what I should say next. I can't see any reason to talk more about Jemell's violence right now since it's a symptom of bigger problems that need to be solved. "So what can I do to help?" I ask.

"I want to change schools," Jemell says. "I want to go to a school with more black kids. I've had it with all them hick whites. I want to go where my girlfriend goes."

Ricky slaps his hands on his thighs. Tina tries to shush him but he won't be silenced. "That girlfriend, that's the one getting him into trouble."

Jemell smirks and rubs his face with both hands. "Like hell, Dad. It was only a thong. It's not like I was out robbing banks or something." I'm obviously a little confused and Tina explains that Jemell and his girlfriend were caught shoplifting a seven-dollar thong at American Eagle.

"If she needed underwear that bad, why couldn't she buy it herself?" asks Ricky.

"It was for, you know, sanitation." Jemell's laughing at his dad's magenta face, the blood vessels in his cheeks bursting.

"But, Jemell," argues Tina, with a hand on her husband's knee, ignoring her son's taunt. "It's not just the stealing. It's also the violence. And we can guess what else is going on. You've got to be careful. You get her pregnant and her father will kill you!"

Jemell smirks. "Yeah, whatever."

"Honestly, I don't understand her dad at all," Ricky says with gritted teeth. "Her father is a single parent, and he is either all strict with her, or he looks the other way. She has a tattoo, and we know she and Jemell are having sex." Jemell rolls his eyes but doesn't argue the truth. "We've tried to talk to him about birth control. But you know how kids are. He just laughs and tells me, 'Look, Dad, I got it all under control.' Except her father is really upset that Jemell's having sex with his daughter. He called us and threatened to kill Jemell if he keeps touching her. That's the word he used: *touching*. Man, they don't prepare you for this crap when you have children."

"Confused yet?" asks Tina, feeling sorry for me having to swim in the chaos of what they call a normal day.

"Yes and no," I say, trying to reassure her that I'm comfortable following their lead. "So what happened? Jemell is still alive?" As I had hoped, we all laugh and the tension breaks.

"Barely," says Ricky. "This is how stupid my boy is. Even with all the trouble he's in, he shoplifts a thong. A seven-dollar red silk thong! And after they're caught, they call both of us to come get them, but we're at work, of course. So they had to call her father." Ricky shakes his head and looks at his son. "Serves you right to have to embarrass yourself like that."

"Sounds like a pretty natural consequence to me." Now it's Jemell's turn to look confused. "You know, you do something and the world dishes up a consequence that fits perfectly." He gets it and smiles a tight-lipped grimace.

"He's got no idea what he's doing," says Tina, her voice cracking slightly with the worry she's holding back.

Maybe it's the novelty of what Jemell did, or the fact that he is still here talking with his parents, but something tells me this boy can turn himself around if we give him what he needs. That's my job. I'm the bull-nosed tugboat that pushes at an ocean liner's bow. I can't tell Jemell what to do, but I may be able to nudge him and his parents along a different course.

"So far, we've stacked violence, racism, drug abuse, theft, and the threat of an unwanted pregnancy on the table. We'd better take these one by one." The easiest is actually the fighting. We decide to help Jemell move schools. At the very least, he won't have to put up with being called the N-word and fewer people will know his reputation for fighting. He'll get to see his girlfriend more often, too, something that I hope will be an incentive for him to avoid suspensions.

As to his being sexually active, the best we can do is to have a conversation about responsible choices, consequences, and protection. Abstinence might be worth considering, but I'm sensing that with Jemell, that ship has sailed. Better to appreciate the rocky shoals we are in and help Jemell navigate the dangers that come with being a sexually active teen. Half an hour later, with a plan in place for a change of school and a conversation with a public health nurse at a teen clinic, Ricky and Tina are more relaxed but still concerned. Jemell leaves my office to make a call on his cell and I have a couple of minutes alone with his parents.

Whispering so Jemell won't hear her, Tina asks, "And the rest of it? What do we do with a boy who gets high and steals?"

"We go one step at a time," I say. "Right now, Jemell needs your help. And he needs to know that despite everything else, you still want to be his parents and are willing to support him as best you can. That doesn't mean sheltering him from the consequences of his behaviour, but it does mean letting him know you are there for him when he needs you."

Ricky and Tina grasp each other by the hand. The thought of what they will have to do if their son makes any more big mistakes scares them. We all know his house arrest will be revoked and he'll be put in jail. It's an awful thought, but they know that a threat without teeth is no threat at all.

There are days with my own children when I doubt I'm doing the right thing. Where once it was me giving them time outs, now there are evenings when they abandon the family willingly, choosing to stay in their rooms, their moodiness hanging in the air as heavy as the stink from their unwashed sports gear. Their self-imposed exile from me is like a knife to my heart every time I think about it.

At times like that, I need proof that using consequences with my children is good child rearing and that in the long run, it will help me stay connected to them. It's those connections that are the topic for our next meeting of the Last Problem Child Group. I explain to everyone that the best evidence I know for this simple truth comes from a rather unlikely source: Stephanie. She's a short, blond-haired girl who I often see sitting quietly in the corner watching television in the secure facility for young offenders that I visit for my work. Despite first impressions, Stephanie is no angel.

She's in custody for murder. Right now, she needs the predictable structure of security doors and the well-trained staff who look after her and a dozen other girls on their living unit. Of course, you'd know Stephanie wasn't like most girls her age once she opened her mouth. She can't say two words before she makes sure one of them begins with an *f*. Not exactly the kind of child you might look to for advice on how we can prevent having more troubled kids. However, for the fourth meeting, I begin with Stephanie's story.

"So, what's been helpful since you came into custody?" I ask her during one of my visits. Her stare is lazy, like a loping camel. I know she will give me little of her attention unless she is convinced I will extend her the courtesy of my patience. Eventually, when I don't go away, she rolls her eyes. Adjusts herself on her chair and smooths her hair. I wait while this pretty prima donna finds her voice.

"My worker. F——in' Tiffany. Only f——in' useful thing in here. Just Tiffany. She's the only person who really stood behind me and actually took enough f——in' time to sit and talk with me."

"What's Tiffany say when you talk together?"

"She tells me I can f——in' still be anything I f——in' want to be. No power trips. Even when I told her, 'I can't do that,' Tiffany tells me, 'Why not? Are you f——in' stupid?' That's why she's cool." The language may be a bit unprofessional, but the connection is solid. Stephanie knows she's met her match, word for word.

A connection with Tiffany isn't all this little girl wants. Ask her what's really important to her, and she'll say the phone calls she makes home to her mother. Her brother and sister, who come to visit once a month. The remote possibility that she'll get to go on a supervised home visit for three hours on Christmas Day. Boil it all down, and the only hope this kid has are the connections that she hasn't yet severed.

To be fair, if I'd met Stephanie eighteen months earlier, I would have been smart to walk on the other side of the street. She was out of control and looking for a victim. She was mean and trying to impress girls who were a lot meaner. It wasn't that much of a surprise that she took a baseball bat and cracked a man's skull when he refused to give her his wallet. Or that she showed little remorse for what she'd done.

"No one ever really gave a f—— about me or where I was. My mother, you probably know, is a f——in' cokehead." Stephanie and her mother yell instead of talking. Every encounter turns into an argument. According to Stephanie, her entire family is pretty "dysfunctional."

Funny as it sounds, Stephanie wants to stay connected with her mother. Sitting there with her, it's as if I'm meeting an overgrown little kid itching to climb onto someone's knee for a cuddle. I think that's what Tiffany provides. A steady stare, the structure of a young-offender housing unit, and just enough attention to convince Stephanie she's still important.

It's not her mother's knee, but there is the occasional hug and the security of knowing someone will both set and enforce the rules.

"I don't always do what I'm f——in' told, but Tiffany understands. Sometimes I just have to go f——in' crazy to make this place work for me. You got to live it to understand. I wouldn't expect a f——in' geek like you to get what I'm saying." I smile at the insult. So does Stephanie. We both know she doesn't really mean it. She just doesn't trust people. If only she'd found someone like Tiffany a little sooner in her life, she might not have killed anyone.

All five parents are listening closely, but it's Tina who jumps forward with a question. "So you're saying Jemell needs us to play the heavy with him. Right?" Tina's question is the same one we all want answered with a definite yes or no.

"Yes," I tell her and watch as she makes a fist and pumps it up and down triumphantly. "But it only works if Jemell knows you're really on his side." Tina's fist opens and she settles back on her chair. "He needs to know that he can push you away sometimes, then pull you close again. Whether our children are five or fifteen, kids are all the same. They're confused about how much they want us in their lives. But they are all just like Stephanie. Pleading with us not to give up on them. Begging for connections with us even as they rebel against the rules we impose."

"So how the heck do we get our kids to accept the rules?" asks Ricky.

"Yeah, my Sadie these days seems to have a mind of her own," says Merlinda.

"Amanda has always had a mind of her own!" adds Katherine.

"All good questions," I say, my hands out in front of me to deflect the barrage of worry hitting me like emotional shrapnel. "When structure and consequences are provided and you make sure your child feels connected to you by insisting he participates in your family, you've already done just about everything you need to do to prevent him from growing up to be a holy terror."

I get up and draw a three-legged stool on the flip chart. "Structure, consequences, and connections with parents — those are the three legs we must stand on to prevent our children from having serious problems. But look closely: it's a three-legged stool I've drawn, so it's always going to be a little unstable. A small change in structure, consequences, or our attachment to our child, and we'll be off balance before we know it."

It's always fun to remind parents just how important they are to their kids. There's lots of ways to prove it, too. "Never doubt your kids share your values," I explain. "In fact, I recently heard about a curious study done with Vietnamese youth who just got electricity in their remote village. Everyone expected the kids, who began watching reruns of *Baywatch*, to become sexually active or abandon the values of their parents and culture altogether. But that didn't happen. Kids watched their new televisions, but what their parents had taught them still put limits on their behaviour. In the competition between parents and Hollywood, parents still won."

Katherine looks reassured. She should be. Parents are so important that when Alan Sroufe and his team of psychologists tracked hundreds of first-born children of mothers living in poverty in Minneapolis, following them until they were twenty years old, they found that they could predict lots of things about a child based on the child's attachment to her parents when she was younger. Poor grades at school and dropping out before completing grade twelve were markers for how well children were cared for when they were three years old. In fact, researchers could predict with 77 percent accuracy which children would drop out in high school based on observations made of the children and their parents even before the children began school. And none of this had to do with the child's IQ. What made the difference was how well the child felt connected to a parent.

"Respond compassionately to your children, and your children will bond with you as surely as peanut butter sticks to the roof of your mouth. But none of this will work, of course, unless you have time to spend with your child." I make this last argument with my finger pointing at each of them one at a time, then pointing back at myself. It is a lesson I need to remember just as much as anyone else who gets frustrated raising their children.

"If I was to tell you that a parent who eats dinner with her child three times a week is far, far less likely to have a teenager who uses drugs, would that be enough for you to tell your youngster to come home for dinner, to turn off the television, and to serve a good hot meal?" We parents don't have to provide such intense relationships every night, but three times a week can be helpful.

I tell the group, "If we really want to make the most of this time together, try laying down some simple rules." I go to the flip chart and begin to write.

What We Shouldn't Do

- Use cellphones or other electronic communication devices for thirty minutes.
- Lecture.
- Yell.

What We Should Do

- Encourage everyone, including parents, to share one thing about their day.
- Say "thank you" to whoever made the meal.
- Insist everyone participate in some aspect of the meal preparation, whether that is cooking or cleaning up.

If a child is five, it's an easy routine to start. Especially if parents realize that the meal could be far more important than any email they answer, meeting they attend, or sporting activity they drive their young child to. A fifteen-year-old who has never had this structure, or who has experienced meals as grabfests, wolfed down in front of the television, with home cooking coming in a bucket, square box, or Styrofoam-lidded container, will be more difficult to convince of the value of sitting down and breaking bread together. There is still time, though, to heal bad habits.

"Remember, your child will one day have his own children. If he's off course, he can be the last child in your family to grow up disconnected to his parents." I wait for everyone to digest this last thought.

"So, think back to when you were little kids. How did your parents make you feel connected? If you didn't feel connected, what did you wish they'd done?"

"I don't think my mom and I ever connected. She'd shoo me out the door when I was just a small thing and threaten me with a beating if I came back before dinner," says Katherine, her cold stare hiding the emotional scars of her neglect.

"That's horrible!" Tina exclaims.

"It wasn't as bad as it sounds. I didn't know any better."

"But what did you want your mother to do?" I ask, certain Katherine isn't really as nonchalant about this as she appears. She shrugs her shoulders.

I can empathize with her feelings of resignation. But I also know that our children want to attach to their caregivers. Research tells us we are hardwired to crave an environment that makes us feel special. Sue Gerhardt, in her book *Why Love Matters*, explores the connection between a baby's brain development and affection. It's a timeless truth. Just think of the emotion that Michelangelo's *Madonna and Child* evokes. The soft, warm gaze of a white marble Mary doting upon the baby Jesus is exactly the gaze we want from a parent or parent substitute.

This need to connect is woven into our body and brains. Peter Fonagy, a professor of psychoanalysis at University College London and an expert on attachment, reminds us the brain is a "social organ." A well-managed baby dances emotionally with her caregivers. If her mother is upset, the baby fusses; if her mother is sad that baby senses her caregiver's despondency and may become withdrawn. In fact, what we know about the lives of babies is that the more we, as parents, maintain our cool and respond to our baby's needs, the more likely the baby is to be well-adjusted and calm. That doesn't mean she won't cry, tantrum, or bite. It just means she learns quickly to self-soothe and return to a state of connected security where all is well in her small world. Fonagy reminds us that our emotionally fragile selves are plastic putty in our parents' hands.

The good news, according to Gerhardt, is that the harm done to one generation isn't necessarily passed on to the next. A damaged child doesn't always grow up to become a parent who is damaged or damages her own children. Even a child with a genetic predisposition toward impulsivity, aggression, or risk taking can avoid becoming a delinquent if the home and school around the child provide a secure attachment and do what's necessary to prevent bad behaviour. In other words, our kids are what we make them.

Even genetics is trumped by environment. Though genetypical risk (for example, a predisposition toward becoming a criminal) can be triggered by maltreatment, genetics is not destiny. Jemell might be a kid with a lot of the genetic markers for problems, but none of that guarantees he'll wind up in jail forever if Tina and Ricky give him the support he needs.

"It's a bit hard to support your kid when he's talking like he's some kind of gangster," says Ricky.

"I hate it when Sadie swears at me. Makes me want to throttle her," Frank adds.

I ask, "Do you ever tell Sadie, Jemell, and Amanda that you expect them to be polite? And that if they want you to do things for them, they have to treat you with more respect?"

Ricky answers, "Mostly we end up screaming at each other. Though not the past week or two," he says. Tina nods in agreement. "We've been standing pretty firmly on that stool. If that's possible. Giving Jemell real clear instructions about what we expect him to do, and what will happen if he breaks the rules. We thought he'd go crazy, but he hasn't. Instead, he keeps a bit more to himself. And he's now the one setting limits on us. I have to knock to enter his room. And he tells me to stop nagging at him if he's not breaking any rules. The other night when I went to see if he'd put his dirty clothes in the laundry, he said he'd wash them himself if he forgets. I'll be damned!"

"That's wonderful," I say. "It's the same with swearing. First we need to avoid swearing at our kids, and second, we need to tell them when their behaviour is inappropriate. I tell my own kids when they dare to say mean things to me that I don't accept that language from anyone else in my life, and I'm not going to accept it from them, either. If they continue being rude, it's not likely I'm going to be cooking anything special for dinner or driving them anywhere. Those are optional on my list of to-do's."

"So, you tell us, Michael, how do we get our kids to connect?" asks Frank. I'm wondering if Sadie has been overly distant since our last conversation.

"I have no simple answer," I reply, "but I suspect everyone in this room has at some point found a way to connect with his or her child."

"Driving," Frank says.

"Pardon?"

"When I'm driving her someplace, it's easier to talk. We're both looking at the road. And we're stuck together for a time. I never say no if she asks for a lift and I have the time to take her somewhere."

"That's clever."

Katherine says, "For me and Amanda it's food. I like to cook, Amanda and I both love to eat. We almost never fight when we're in the kitchen. It's just finding the time or getting her to turn off the damn television. But once we've got a project, like Christmas baking, then we're okay."

"So when your children are depending on you, and you're not in an intense situation where you're grilling them with questions about school or their friends or anything else, no mini lectures, then you feel connected? And they do, too? The trick is to learn from those times when your relationship works and do more of the same."

Heads nod and everyone's eyes dart up and to the left, a sure sign they are thinking back to good times with their kids. I have the same thoughts about my own children. Month-long trips overseas for my research, with them tagging along. Days spent snowboarding at the small hill an hour from our home. The Sunday morning pancake breakfasts I like to cook.

We spend the rest of the evening telling stories about times we felt connected to our children. I ask questions that help us get to the nitty-gritty details of how those connections are made solid. When Katherine says she and Amanda like to go shopping together on Saturday afternoons, wandering through the expensive downtown boutiques, I ask her how she avoids arguing with Amanda when she wants to buy something that Katherine can't afford.

"Oh sure, that happens every now and then, but mostly I tell her to get herself a good education and earn lots of money, then she can buy those things for herself. Then we go get an ice cream or one of those fancy iced-coffee things at Starbucks. She knows I can't afford expensive things. But every now and then we find a bargain rack with everything 70 percent off. When that happens, I let her choose one thing she likes. Or sometimes she helps me find something for myself. She likes that, too."

"There's a lot of wisdom in what you're saying," I tell her. Katherine has managed to make her daughter feel special, a little more adult-like. She's treated her respectfully by explaining the family's finances and letting Amanda take some responsibility for what she can and cannot buy.

It makes me warm inside thinking about them wandering those stores together, and I'm not someone who likes to shop.

There are other suggestions, too. I write them on the flip chart so we'll remember them.

Ways To Feel Connected To Your Child

- Go out for a meal as a family. The kids will love it, and you're less likely to argue in a public place.
- Go to a movie together. It's two hours of contact without the pressure to talk. Afterward, there's the chance for you each to say what you thought of the film.
- Invite your children's friends over for a meal. Your children will appreciate the gesture and you'll be able to find out a little more about what's on your child's mind and the minds of his friends.
- Let your child plan a trip. Even a preadolescent can help develop a travel itinerary. Children are more likely to want to travel with you and enjoy the time spent together when they have some say over the destination.
- Visit extended family. Your kids will have a better sense of who you are as a real person as they listen to stories about your past. They may also feel more connected to their entire family.
- Play a game together. Board games or sports both work just fine. Focusing on friendly competition lets you spend time together without having to talk about problems. Strategically creating teams is a great way to help repair broken relationships.
- Make yourself easily available. Rather than sitting in a separate room, take your magazine and read someplace where the kids can wander in and find you, or even better, seek them out and do your reading next to them.
- Text. It's a great way to keep connected with your tech-savvy children and they'll appreciate the anonymity of speak-

ing to you without having to admit they're answering a call from their mother or father.

- Volunteer together. Find something that interests your child, like the environment or animal rights, and plan a time to do some fundraising door-to-door, participate in a walkathon, or help an organization in another way as a family.
- Watch your child play a sport (if she is athletic) or go listen to her perform in her band (if she is musical). The support will be appreciated and it will give you both something positive to talk about afterward.
- Read with your child. It's not just good for the child's grades at school — it also creates a special time for the two of you together.
- Say good night to your child every night. Even better, give him a hug no matter how old he is. It's a comforting way for a child to end a day, even one during which you were arguing with each other.

Our list grows and grows until it's nearing time to leave. I ask everyone to consider doing a piece of homework. "Choose one activity from all the ones we've discussed tonight and find the time this week to do that activity with your 'problem' child. Let's see what happens." I promise to do the same with my own children.

Everyone nods and I pass out a summary cue card, which they slip into their wallets and purses.

Katherine waves a hasty goodbye. "I've got some things to tell Amanda," she says, and is off.

"That was a heavy session. Like beef stew. I feel like I'll be digesting all night," Frank tells me. Merlinda has been unusually quiet this evening. She is standing not so patiently at the door waiting for him.

"Will I see you both next week?"

"Sure," Frank says and glances at his wife. She stays put. "This stuff with Sadie just wears us down, but we're committed. That was helpful tonight. Gave me hope. You know, reminded me that we still have some good times together now and then."

Things Our Children Need
3. Parent-Child Connections

- Our children want to know that their problems are theirs to solve, and that parents are available to help them when they're needed.
- Our children really do want connections with their parents, but those connections will look very different at each age and stage of development.
- Our children appreciate the effort their parents make to connect with them. Parents need to remember what they've done right in the past and do more of the same in the future.

"It will get better. I'm sure of it. She's got two great parents," I say, trying to sound enthused. Frank reaches out and shakes my hand but doesn't say anything. He looks worried as we loosen our grip.

Chapter 9

The Fourth Thing Children Need — Lots and Lots of Relationships

Former U.S. president Bill Clinton likes to remind us that we live in an interdependent world. What I do affects many others, who in turn, affect me. And yet, still people go hungry and children lack anti-malarial mosquito nets and AIDS patients don't get the medicines we know will dramatically extend their lives.

Such weakness in our ability to look after one another is never because of a shortage of good ideas. Clinton says our problem is that we so seldom figure out *how* to put good ideas into practice. It's the *how* question that prevents us from acting in the best interests of others and ourselves.

I'm in my office two hours before our fifth session trying to figure out how I'll explore with the group what their children need from them once they've calmed their kids with structure, consequences, and connections.

What next?

What do we actually give our kids once we have them perched on that three-legged stool, understanding that they have limits and responsibilities, as well as our love? I know there's an answer. For a moment I'm inspired by Aaron Wildavsky, the American political scientist who encouraged a trial and error optimism, arguing against the precautionary principles of those who would slow the advance of new technology. "What we try to do depends to some degree on what we can do," he said. I have seen kids leave problems behind. It therefore follows that these three families can help their children do the same. But how?

I sit staring at my computer screen. I slouch forward in my ergonomic chair. Even it can't stop me from feeling the burden of my task. My breath is short. I need to straighten up or else my thoughts will fog. But I'm procrastinating and let myself daydream. Relish the sense that something, liquid and shimmering, is just lying there on the edge of thought. It's big, waiting ...

My eyes close and there's Ricky, standing above me, inviting me to change seats with him. He wants me to sit among the group. "What about you?" he asks, a sausage-sized finger pointing down at my chest. "We're pouring our guts out and we don't even know how many kids you have. Or if you're married. Or what your father and mother did to screw you up, just like the rest of us."

I swirl down the vortex. I remember my mother for the beatings, but my father left me with nothing. I dream him now into a ripe old man. A wrinkled tomato oozing its rotted insides.

There was so much silence.

I think of that strange play on words, "nothing is enough." If you are unhappy, you think about all that you are missing. Nothing then is ever enough to satisfy the deeper longing. But if you are all grown up, successful, past the compulsion of always needing to prove yourself, then you don't need very much at all. You are the Buddhist in the cave, on retreat. A meagre bowl of food, your sustenance. Nothing (or almost nothing) *is* enough. I wish I could feel satisfied like that. But my father left so many unanswered questions that I never feel full.

Ricky's apparition is right. I am as much of this group as anyone else who attends. I may have answers, but they are only a cover for the many questions I still have that I can't speak to.

That's when it hits me. The answer to "what next?" It has been there in front of me the whole time. It was there in the coffee shop. It was there when Sadie told me about the baby she wants.

What's next is always what's available. We cope by taking advantage of the opportunities that are presented to us.

My father coped as best he could with what he had. The bastard. I blame him for not trying harder. But then, I'm not him. I went looking for the things I needed to have a problem-free and flourishing life. He likely did, too, only with less success.

I pull myself back into my body, straighten, and breathe deeply. "I've got a feeling," I begin humming, "that tonight's gonna be a good night...." I start typing madly. The more the Last Problem Child Group helps me understand why I survived, the more it will work for those who are trusting me to help them.

The answer to their success is hidden in my own.

Everyone is here except Merlinda. Frank tells me she's exhausted and running a fever. They were up most of last night worrying about Sadie, who didn't come home until two in the morning. "She was at a friend's," he says, "with her cellphone off. On a school night!" I reassure him we'll talk about these sorts of behaviours during the group tonight.

Katherine says quietly, "My God, she's young for that kind of thing," and both Frank and I know she is thinking about Amanda, who will soon be the same age as Sadie. Frank settles back on his chair.

"Does this mean you didn't get a chance to do something nice together?" I ask.

"Oh, we did. We went to a movie. Something with zombies. It was disgusting, of course, but you know, it seemed to help a little. She even sat with us for a while afterward at McDonald's, which was her choice. For a moment ..." He can't complete his sentence. He's too overwhelmed with what he can't admit he feels. We all sit in witness to his pain.

"Amanda and I had a good time, too," Katherine says, hoping she can take the focus off Frank. It's a lovely gesture. "We cooked, for a fundraiser at her school. It was for earthquake victims. Amanda was so proud when she brought five dozen cookies to school the next morning. She even came home right away after school and phoned me at work like I asked her to. It was, well, like a miracle." Even Frank is smiling now. Katherine's experience gives us all hope.

"I'm afraid Jemell and I were mostly fighting this week," says Tina. "I thought about the homework, but by the time we got over being angry, there was no time."

"What about giving him a hug?" I ask.

There's a strange pause. Tina looks at Ricky. "I was so upset," she says, "with his mouthing off at me, I couldn't."

"But I did," says Ricky. "It was weird. I just went down to his room in the basement, told him, 'I know you're angry, but you're still my son and I love you,' and then I gave him a hug. Well, sort of a hug. You know, put my arm around his shoulder. I was sure he was going to pull away, but he didn't."

Not bad, I'm thinking. They're making progress, putting money in an emotional bank account with their kids. There are still going to be problems, but at least they'll have some good times to fall back on.

Shifting gears, I tell the group, "Tonight, I want to talk about the first of six specific things that families like yours have shown me are necessary to raise resilient kids. Each of the six depends on how well we've provided children with structure, consequences, and connections." Everyone nods, which makes me feel confident to continue.

"Tonight, then, I'd like to talk about the relationships your kids need, not just with you, which we talked about last week, but with many other adults and their peers. To start, though, I'm wondering if you have read Malcolm Gladwell's *Outliers*?" Only Frank raises his hand. "That's okay. Everyone else may want to get a copy after tonight."

Outliers is a book about how people succeed. Invariably, those who are the most successful are the beneficiaries of hidden advantages and extraordinary opportunities. It makes a difference where and when we grow up, the culture we belong to, and the stories handed down to us about what success means and how one achieves it. Gladwell wants his readers to understand that what people are like on the inside isn't nearly as important as where they are from and when they were born. It's what he calls the "machinery of achievement" that determines our life course.

When I look at the parents in front of me, or myself in a mirror, I know Gladwell is right. There are lots of parts to that machinery but none more important than the relationships our children find as they grow up.

I thought of that machinery when I met Grace, a fourteen-year-old living in rural India. She is deaf but has had the remarkably good fortune of having been provided with access to a school that teaches sign language and a regular academic curriculum for children with physical challenges.

A day student at the school, she has parents who care enough about her to ensure she gets an education.

At school, the atmosphere is warm. Small classes of children with similar impairments work through their lessons. I watch as they walk the compound in tight groups of friends, the girls holding hands and laughing at the boys who try to get their attention. The boys' gangly arms and legs remind me of the pubescent teens in my own neighbourhood. It's only the words they try to speak that are awkward, strange utterances that they themselves cannot hear. They leave with memories of laughter and playground friendship. But there are also responsibilities. The older girls like Grace must look after the younger children, something done without hesitation. It's a rite of passage for them, a way of making their contribution. To those who rely upon them, they are not disabled, broken children, but competent young women with something to give back.

It's the same for Grace at home, where her mother is ill with uterine cancer. Grace is worried about her but buffers herself from the anxiety that threatens to overwhelm her by seeking solace kneeling on a pew at a nearby church. It's an interesting choice considering she isn't Christian. Her name, Grace, was given to her by the nuns. Her real name is Neerja. Through an interpreter, she tells me that at home she likes to grow flowers and dance to the heavy beat of a drum vibrating up through the soles of her feet.

If it wasn't for her school and the caring nuns who run it, one wonders what would have become of Neerja. Grace (she accepts humbly her new name) wants others to know her for her creativity and intelligence. She wants them to be mirrors for her smiles. She may never leave the security of these connections. Grace tells me she wants to grow up and be a sign language teacher. She likes the little children who follow her. She has found within her school relationships that feed her, that make her feel every bit as whole as the children who can hear the cuckoos in the trees above her head.

Gladwell would likely be intrigued by Grace if he met her.

"Here is a young woman," I explain, "who, to the best of her ability, is taking control of the machinery. That is Gladwell's point — that we can influence the likelihood individuals will succeed if we change the weave of circumstance around them. Give a child a school, friendships, a parent (even one who is ill) that need the child's care, and a role that makes the child feel needed, and most children will do well, no matter where they are growing up."

Katherine asks, "Is it the school that makes the difference for Grace, or the teachers?" It's a good question. "Amanda was happy to bring in those cookies, but still, there are plenty of days I can't get her to go to school. And it's a good school, too."

"What do you think, Frank?" I ask, trying to bring more voices into the conversation with Katherine.

"Well, it sounds like it's the school being there that makes the difference. But really, isn't it the teachers who are important? I think that's what Sadie is looking for. Some adults to tell her she's special. She's too old to hear that just from Merlinda and me. And I don't want her hearing it from some sex-crazed boy. I want her to have adults in her life she can trust."

"Yes, exactly," I say. "That machinery Gladwell is talking about includes lots of things, like schools. But in my experience, the first and most important thing is the people our children connect to. Their parents, of course, the other adults in their lives next, and then their peers."

Ricky looks confused. "You put their peers third. I think if you asked Jemell, he'd say his crew were a lot more important to him than Tina and me."

"For some things. But in general, if we're talking about raising a next generation of children who have no problems, it's still us adults who count more. Grandparents, teachers, coaches, mentors, Big Brothers and Big Sisters, even the police. We shape our children's self-esteem and the opportunities they have to prove themselves. When they look at us, we are mirrors. Like we talked about last week, parents influence the stories children tell about themselves. But so, too, do other adults and children's peers."

"I like that I'm my kid's storyteller," says Ricky. "But, I'll tell you, if Jemell doesn't get it together soon, the story I'll write for him won't be a bedtime story. It'll be *Friday the 13th*!"

We all laugh at Ricky's exaggeration, but we all know and fear the influence peers can have on our children. I'm reminded of a Native American tale about a grove of very sick trees in a diseased forest. A few of those trees ask for help from a kind-hearted arborist who takes them away from their forest home and plants them temporarily in fertile gardens where they blossom. Eventually, though, homesick, they ask to return to their forest, which is still troubled. It's not long before the now healthy trees are reinfected and their capacity to cope overwhelmed.

As Jude Simpson, a family life educator in New Zealand, likes to say, "Show me your friends and I'll tell you who you are."

Of course, we know that delinquent youth are more likely to hang out with other delinquent youth, and that youth who drop out of school are more likely to spend time among other school leavers. But what we don't know is which comes first. It's a classic chicken-and-egg problem. Does dropping out leave them with the time to spend with equally troubled kids, or does their interest in those kids make them think, "Hey, dropping out is a good thing to do"? I think it's both. Kids are desperate to feel like they belong.

"Is that what Sadie is looking for, then?" asks Frank. "We tell her she's special. Why does she need to be sexually active to know it's true?"

"I suspect Sadie is looking to find connections with lots of different people. It's not that you aren't giving her lots of what she needs, but she could be telling us she wants to be in the presence of those who think she's older. Fortunately, as our kids grow, they also grow in their capacities to attach. But you and Merlinda are doing the right thing by continuing to offer Sadie a relationship. I suspect she'd be a lot more out of control if she didn't have you there supporting her."

"I really worry what will become of her if we ease up."

"You shouldn't give up. No matter what happens."

"Are you saying she still might make bad decisions?" Frank asks. I know what he wants me to say, but I can't lie.

"She still might, Frank. But I can guarantee you, with you and Merlinda a part of her life, the decisions she makes will not be as bad as the ones she could have made." He nods and I change my focus slightly. "Finding a mentor is also important to our children's healthy development. The more adults in their lives, the better."

In the 1990s, John Laub and Robert Sampson at Harvard University tracked down five hundred delinquent boys who grew up in the Boston area during the Depression. They were originally part of a study that was trying to predict which boys would turn out well and which badly. The original authors of the study, Sheldon and Eleanor Glueck, followed boys from two reformatories until they were thirty-two years old. Laub and Sampson found records of these men when they were nearing seventy. Half had died, but the stories gathered from those still living tell of lives that either left crime behind, remained criminal forever, or zigzagged in and out of conflict with the law.

Those who survived the best almost always reported good relationships with someone who cared about them: a neighbour, coach, drill sergeant, spouse, or parent. They also said they'd found for themselves a meaningful place in a community that accepts them.

"So you're saying our kids really want healthy relationships with some adult who cares about them and will mentor them to go straight."

"Yes, Frank. But I wouldn't say they *want* relationships. I'd say they *need* relationships! We adults can't give up on our kids just because they tell us to eff-off. We need to stay put and help them."

It's getting late, but before the group leaves, I have one last story to share. One I hope will offer them some hope that their children are earnestly seeking adults with whom they can form healthy relationships.

I tell them, "Some years ago I met a youth worker who did twelve-hour shifts at a downtown shelter for homeless youth. One evening, a couple of regular clients brought with them a young woman who, from the looks of her, had been sleeping on people's couches or on the street for many days. She needed a shower and some new clothes. If her appearance was shabby, it was nothing compared to the foulness of the language she used. This was a seasoned street survivor who the staff suspected was likely caught up in swapping sex for drugs or a place to stay. It wasn't clear why she'd come to the shelter that night, but they guessed something bad must have happened that had scared her enough to let her guard down and accept their help.

"All evening they put up with her insults. She thought they were 'f——in' retards' when they asked her if she needed help putting sheets on her bed. The television was blaring and then blared louder when she turned it up. It was like watching a two-year-old trying to run the world. Eventually, showing the grace of a stern but loving parent, the staff managed to get her to settle down. She fell asleep in a dorm with a dozen other girls.

"The next morning she was groggy but had thankfully showered and helped herself to a new pair of underwear and jeans from the donation bin behind the kitchen. Her long, wet hair was an uncombed, straggly mess that fell into her empty cereal bowl. In addition to putting boxes of cereal on the table, the staff made an effort to provide some fresh fruit and there was real milk donated by a local dairy. Most of the kids were quietly eating, except for the young woman with the wet hair. Her attitude was still alive and well. 'What kind of f——in' place is this, anyway?' she shouted loudly enough so that everyone could hear. 'There's no Cocoa Puffs. Just bran crap.'

"I'm not sure quite what made him do it, but the youth worker who told me this story went to the kitchen and took a five-dollar bill from the petty cash. With the other staff covering for him, he ran down the street to a Quick Mart and bought a small box of chocolate-flavoured corn puffs. Then he ran back and, without saying a word, strolled by the young woman and placed the cereal in front of her. He never knew if she smiled or frowned. He just kept walking straight back to the kitchen and resumed his chores.

"The young woman never said thank you or stopped mouthing off at the staff. She left when the shelter shut its doors for the day, with an invitation to return anytime she liked. She didn't return that evening. Nor the next. Three weeks later, however, she came back. She had the same pissy attitude and the same complaints about breakfast. This time, though, she wasn't given any Cocoa Puffs.

"She left again but returned a week later and soon became a regular. Two months after her first visit, she asked to meet with a nurse who came to the shelter a few times a week. The young woman was pregnant and had contracted herpes.

"It's hard to build these bridges for children back into their communities and families. But as Reed Larson, a professor of human and community development at the University of Illinois, reminds us, 'It is easier to think about moulding clay than about helping the clay mould itself.' That youth worker did something small, but very special, when he showed that young woman that staff at the shelter cared about her enough to give her what she really needed."

I pull from my binder a list of tips that I've learned throughout my career from people like that youth worker and pass each group member a copy.

"When I think of ways to build caring relationships between adults and children, I think of strategies like these."

Things Children Tell Me They Really Want from Adults

- A child wants adults to catch him doing something fabulously well and to be applauded for his success.
- A child wants not just her parents but lots of adults to notice when she behaves in ways that tell us she isn't a problem child.
- A child wants adults to talk about his problems as things that are separate from the child ("I see you're having a problem with learning math" instead of "*You* can't learn math").
- A child wants a chance to make a contribution to his family, school, and community. Volunteer activities ensure a child sees himself as competent, while gathering around him peers and adults who will see him as someone special.
- A child needs to know that she is expected to do her best, whatever that best is. A child who doesn't believe anyone cares how well she does is a child who will feel lost and hopelessly alone.
- A child wants to feel accepted by others. A child who knows he is welcome in his family, at his school, and in his community will most likely take advantage of the opportunities he finds there to belong. Adults don't have to accept a child's problem behaviour to still accept the child as someone worthy of love.

"I think that's it for tonight. You may want to think about all the special adults and positive peers with whom your child has a relationship. Next time, we'll talk about the identities that they help our children create."

Before we break, I hand out the evening's cue card.

Things Our Children Need
4. Lots and Lots of Relationships

- Our children live in interdependent worlds that bring them the possibility of lots of supportive relationships. Our job as parents is to help them nurture these connections.
- Our children need to feel they are needed and important. They need people in their lives who make them feel this way.
- Adults remain important to children throughout their childhood and adolescence.
- Our children need adults and peers who can help them build bridges back into their communities when their behaviour has made them outsiders.

Katherine reads the cue card carefully before putting it in her purse. Tina and Ricky get up quickly and leave. Frank grabs his coat from the wall hook and signals for me to join him in the corner. Katherine looks our way and is about to approach but decides instead to just wave good night.

I wave back, making a mental note to phone her tomorrow, then turn to Frank. "How *is* Sadie?" I ask, anticipating the conversation.

"Not so good. We give her structure, like you said, and she runs off."

"Is she safe?" My rushed words betray me. I'm obviously worried.

"She just heads over to her aunt Maggie's. She's a complete nut. Everything is politics over there. Sadie's safe enough, but her aunt tells her about the apocalypse. Like it's a good thing. She had her tubes tied when she was twenty-two so she could reduce her carbon footprint. She was sure then she never wanted kids. Now she has Sadie to twist around."

It's late and I'm afraid if I ask for more details, I'll be here for another hour at least. Sadie's safe, that's what's important. And she's got someone who cares about her, politics aside.

"We'll talk about this in group. It will come together. Honestly." I'm pleading with Frank to believe me. Or maybe still trying to convince myself.

Even as I move Frank toward the door, he reminds me of someone desperate for food. His hand is outstretched, not to shake goodbye but to pull me out into the night with him. I can't give him quick answers. He is a good parent with a challenging child. Sadie will do all right if all the adults in her life keep working together. They provide a web of relationships for a confused little girl who is quickly becoming a recalcitrant young woman. Spiky hair, piercings, and an interest in sex that is going to lead her down some dangerous rabbit holes where childhood fantasies are not quite what they seemed. The real world is not MTV and glamorous boys who will admire what's in your trunk. It's boys like Jemell who will open the trunk, raid the treasure, and leave. Pirates, not princes.

Neither Frank nor I want to speak our thoughts out loud. After all, we're both fathers with daughters.

I walk home to clear my thoughts. Tonight was grease to memories. They slide forward through time. Like each parent in the group, I remember finding lots of people who made up for what I didn't get at home.

When I was fifteen and ran away, I went to my English teacher's apartment. He used to hold rehearsals for the school play on Sunday afternoons at his place. My first year in high school, I played a dead body in a Greek tragedy. By my graduating year, I had the lead. Mr. Vineberg's house had always been a place where I felt different, like I could be anyone I wanted to be.

I knocked, and he quickly invited me in. I was so upset I was shaking. I can't remember anything he said, only that he listened, then told me I had to call my parents and let them know where I was. I refused, of course, but he insisted. Then he listened some more.

The listening was important, though what really counted was that I knew he believed in me. When I looked into his eyes, what I saw was hope. He set the bar high for me and expected me to achieve great things. When I handed him my first English essay in grade ten, a book report on Dostoevsky's *Crime and Punishment*, he gave me an A-plus. That was an almost-unheard-of mark at a time when grades weren't inflated to lamely prop up kids' fledgling self-esteem or make teachers feel more secure in their jobs.

It was a great moment, holding that paper with his comments on the front. Except then he told me, "Now that I know what you can do, that's the last A you'll likely get from me." He held to that promise. He no longer marked me the same as he did all the other students. When I finally achieved an A on my final assignment, I knew just how special my work really was. And how special *I* was.

Chapter 10

The Fifth Thing Children Need — A Powerful Identity

Dear Dad,

My apologies for writing you much too late, but I was thinking of you yesterday. I was lying partially anaesthetized on a hospital gurney as doctors performed a colonoscopy. I watched on a television screen the snaking camera wheedle its way up my rectum and, finally, after a magnificent contortion worthy of an Olympic diver, explore the pristine territory of my laxative-cleansed colon.

You never told me about your experience of colonoscopies, or biopsies and barium enemas, either. You only hinted years ago that you were having "procedures" done. There is nothing routine about having a camera snake up your butt or watching as a bright light illuminates the sausage-skin membrane of your sphincter.

Thankfully, there were no cancerous tumours. Just a few irritable-looking hemorrhoids that the python invading me opened its jaws and bit. It was like watching the movie Alien *or maybe Jules Verne in his submersible, twenty thousand millimetres under my skin.*

The doctors had asked me several months earlier, "Any

history of bowel disease or cancer?" and I told them about you. I was embarrassed that I couldn't tell them exactly what you died from. "My father never told me what was wrong," I explained. They knitted their eyebrows and proceeded to the next question.

Once again, you've left me with empty spaces that I am alone to fill. Not just questions about your identity (whose child were you really?) but also questions about what diseases I should fear. And what I am predisposed to become.

Lying on the gurney, I remembered your kidney stones when I was much younger and still living at home. You passed them in the night, howling with pain. Then there was your cancerous kidney a few years later. I worry you may have left me something after all, more dangerous than your neglect, more intimate than memories of your wood shop.

I couldn't help but be a little angry at you yesterday. You died of something that is coiled slumbering on a branch of my genetic tree but you never called to warn me. Sorry if I sound bitter. It's just that watching my insides glow fleshy-white with a cross-hatch of red veins, I was worrying about death.

My death, not yours.

I score a triple homerun before our next session. Three runaways, and all of them back home again. Amanda was the first to disappear. When I phoned Katherine late in the afternoon the day after our last session, she told me Amada hadn't come home yet from school. Katherine didn't go looking for her. "I knew she would come home when she wanted to come home. I can't keep chasing her." Her voice was weary from tears that had been long shed and dried. "I miss her, Michael, I really miss her." And then she sighed heavily into the phone. "She's my little girl and I just want her close. Is that too much to ask?"

I called back a few hours later. Amanda had come home and Katherine had given her a long hug and then cried, her eyes pressed against the girl's hair. Katherine said Amanda had tried at first to squirm away, then held her mother close and said she was sorry.

I asked Katherine if she and Amanda wanted to come in and talk. She surprised us both, I think, when she said no. "The group is helping a lot. But Amanda doesn't want to see a counsellor, and I don't want to force her. I think with your help, I can handle this. At least until she's older and chooses to go see a counsellor herself." I completely agreed. I've always preferred to help a parent support her child than to appear like a magician and make it look like I'm the reason kids get better. Katherine can handle this herself if the other parents in the group and I help her find what she needs to parent well.

Sadie, meanwhile, slept over at a friend's without telling her parents. They were livid when they found her Sunday morning. They said she looked like she had been drinking. There were apparently no parents at the friend's home the night before, either. Just eight unsupervised girls. Sadie insisted she'd told her parents where she was going. The worst part was when she started screaming at them, saying they were treating her like a baby. "I'm thirteen! I'm not a child anymore." The more she screamed and tantrummed, the more childlike she looked. Despite the blow-up, Frank and Merlinda were so happy to know their daughter was still alive they forgot to be angry.

Jemell was another matter. He hadn't been going to school, hanging out instead at the mall. His mid-term report card made it clear that he had better start attending regularly or else he would have to repeat his year. If Merlinda and Frank were scared, and Katherine sad, Tina trumped them both with an explosion of anger that she directed at her son. "I'm gonna kill that kid," she shouted into the phone.

I worried she might. She'd slapped him before. Ricky worried Jemell would take a swing at his mother. If that happened, everything would change, and not for the better. Jemell might be charged, and that would mean more involvement with the police and a spiral down a path far too many young black men travel in this country. Ricky wanted to keep his son from becoming another statistic. Tina, meanwhile, wanted her boy to mind her rules and pay attention to his studies.

I could do little else than listen to each parent and remind each of them to enforce structure, tie consequences to actions, and model the behaviour they want from their children (which meant not screaming at them, hitting them, or giving them the cold shoulder). If they did that, they might keep a relationship and exert a little influence over their kids' lives.

"Never doubt your child needs you," I told them each in turn. "They are trying to figure out who they are. A grown-up? A child? The smart kid or the rebel? They're looking for an identity, something to say proudly about themselves."

I knew this to be true. Even in my most desperate moments, I never stopped needing my parents to notice that I was a child worth loving. The trouble was they never seemed to understand that their role was to play the appreciative audience to my stage performance of the youngster growing up quickly.

I think they thought I was there to applaud them rather than the other way around.

"Try this," I tell the group. "With a partner, stand with your hands outstretched, palm to palm but not touching. Katherine, you can be my partner. We'll have the women be the leaders." Frank and Ricky groan. "Katherine, Merlinda, Tina, think of each of us guys as your mirrors. Whatever you do, we have to do. Smile, blink, wave your hand, walk … you choose."

Thirty seconds later, after Katherine has made me into a pretzel, I tell the group, "Revenge time! Switch roles." It's the women's turn to groan. The men lead and the women become football players and hulking apes as we fellas tease them with a vengeance.

Once we're all laughing, I ask everyone to go back to the first position, with their palms raised, facing one another. I tell them, "This time, without deciding who is going to lead and who is going to follow, and without giving each other any kind of verbal or non-verbal clue, just start!"

They look confused. There is a moment of nervous laughter, then magically, one pair after another begins an unchoreographed ballet. Katherine looks at me for what seems like several minutes before she finally waves her right index finger. I wave back and twitch my thumb.

She follows with her thumb, then she frowns and turns her head to the left. I frown and follow her lead, turning to my right, and begin to walk. It makes us look like we're about to tango and she feigns an exaggerated swoon, her right hand across her brow. I'm about to follow when I realize swooning will likely put my back out, and we both end up embarrassed at how silly we look.

Back in our seats, I explain, "Being with our kids and helping them find a powerful identity for themselves is a lot like the third part of that game. Our kids are negotiating with us to find something powerful to say about themselves. They want an identity that convinces others they are someone special and worth liking."

"So we have to accept whatever they want to be? Follow their lead?" asks Ricky. "Most days, Jemell wants to be some sort of punk-ass gangster with lots of bling. You're not saying I have to accept that, are you?"

"No, not really. We can direct our children toward identities that we like. If you know Jemell likes fighting, then obviously he could end up a brawler constantly getting into trouble with the law. But that identity as someone who fights could also be useful as a hockey player, in a martial arts competition, or even as a lawyer if he agreed to put aside his fists in favour of his mouth. We are like coaches when it comes to helping our kids find something powerful to say about themselves. We can suggest things they can try, but it's still our kids who are on the field making the plays."

"I don't feel like Jemell listens to my advice at all."

"I know it can feel like that, and more than one coach has gotten furious with his team for not doing what they're told. But like it or not, you're on the sidelines. Of course, you can stop being a coach and be an audience instead."

"Whoa, now. Mirrors? Coaches? Identities? Now I'm an audience?" Tina is waving surrender. "Slow down, please."

"Sorry. Let me explain. Your kids are looking to you to help them find something good to say about themselves."

"I get that," says Tina.

"Just like us adults, they want to walk down the street and strut! Think John Travolta in *Saturday Night Fever* and you get the idea. We can make suggestions, but let's face it, we really don't know what it will take for our children to get noticed in their world. Most days, working with children like Jemell, I feel as obsolete as a rotary dial phone. That means all I can really do is sit back and be an audience to my kid's performance. I can applaud or boo depending on what I see."

"So we don't offer unconditional love?" asks Katherine.

"You can still love the child but abhor the child's behaviour. Just as I can like the personality of a contestant on *American Idol* but think his singing sucks. No matter what awful thing my child does, I want him to know I love him, but that doesn't mean I approve of all the choices he makes, nor the identities he chooses that go along with the decisions he makes. I would be pretty disappointed if my own kid dropped out of school. He sure wouldn't get my applause or support. However, I would understand if he decided not to go to university. As long as he did something else that was respectable, I'd be the first to applaud."

"You still have that influence?" Frank asks, sliding down in his seat. "Most days, I'm not sure Sadie hears anything we say."

"I'm not so sure I believe that, Frank. We know a fair bit about the way people form identities, especially kids. And what we know reminds us that parents are very important to their kids. At least we can be when we provide our children with the means to put powerful, safe identities into practice."

I pass out a list of questions we can ask our kids that can help them discover a positive and powerful identity for themselves. One by one, I read them out loud.

- When you look in the mirror, who do you see?
- Is who you see a powerful person or a weak person?
- Who do you think others — your family, friends, teachers — see when they look at you? Do they see the same person you see or someone different?
- Among your friends, what kind of person is the most respected?
- How are you the same as other people in your peer group?
- How are you different? What makes you special or unique?
- How comfortable are you being different? Are there advantages or disadvantages to being a little different from others?

- Being who you are, what can you do that you couldn't do if you were someone else?

Frank interrupts. "What do you mean by that last question?"

"I mean, the more Sadie plays the bad girl, the rebel, the I'm-all-grown-up-and-ready-to-make-my-own-decisions type of kid, the more she gets to do things that she couldn't do if she was a kid who was better behaved."

"You're right about that. The way she acted on the weekend meant she got to stay out all night at her friend's. We'd never have agreed to that if she'd asked."

"Exactly. The more she plays the bad kid, the more she gets what she wants. All the freedom and no responsibility. She's not really looking at an adult in the mirror, is she? She's looking at a little kid all dressed up in an adult disguise. The trick is to offer her another identity that is adult-like without all the danger of the childish adult she has become."

"I'll have to think about that," says Frank.

"Well, I don't," says Katherine. "I know exactly what Michael means. My mother treated me like a young woman. Gave me tons of responsibility. But she never said thank you or nothing. She just expected me to act like I was older."

"That didn't do you any good, did it?"

"Damn right it didn't. Just made me hate responsibility."

"My own research on this suggests that it's not enough to just hand our children a powerful adult-like identity. They also need, and want, an attachment to us and responsibility for themselves and others. Our job," I explain, "is to help children like Sadie feel that they are powerful people worthy of our respect. We can do this by offering them what I call *substitute identities*. Ways they can behave that are both safe and powerful."

"I don't know what my mother could have offered me," says Katherine. "I decided on my own that I would leave home early and be responsible for myself. I remember looking in the mirror the day after I left home and thinking that my life was all my own now. I wasn't afraid like I thought I'd be. I was proud, though. While all my friends were still at home, I was independent."

"There are lots of older teens and young adults who could use that same experience. They would benefit from being given more responsibility for themselves rather than being treated like oversized children." The group laughs and I take that as my cue to finish reading the questions that I handed them.

- If you were someone else and behaved differently, would you still have friends?
- If you did change your behaviour, how would others see you?
- Would anyone insist that you go back to who you were before?
- What can I do to help you be someone with fewer problems and many more strengths?

"Imagine you are an elementary school teacher working with grade five girls who tell you that they sometimes purposely make mistakes on tests to appear less intelligent than they really are. Believe it or not, even in a world where 60 percent of university students are women, girls are still getting the message that it's not cool to be brainy. As their teacher, you could challenge the girls and advise them to talk back to silly boys who say that girls are better when their 'hair outweighs their brains.' But that won't necessarily create a change in their behaviour. The girls will change only when lots of people, especially their peers, make a big fuss over them when they get high marks. Each individual girl has to become an active part of the audience for all the other girls in her class. Add the affirmation of parents, a guidance counsellor, a female astronaut who comes and speaks to the girls, and a television show that celebrates a brainy girl as its hero, and maybe there will be enough noise to silence the voices that tell girls they can't be intellectually gifted and cool at the same time."

It's Ricky's turn to interrupt. "So the kids are looking for something? How did you put it? Something powerful to say about themselves. Tina and I are good people. We've done all right in life. Why does Jemell want to be another screwed-up kid when he could be more like us?"

"Hmm. I'm not sure I know. But I could guess. You see, identities have to make sense to kids. It's like they're hunters. Or maybe gatherers. I don't know which, but I hear the kids tell me they are looking for some way to convince themselves, and everyone else, they are adult-like little people. That means sometimes proving they are just as smart as us parents, and other times throwing everything we believe right back in our faces and insisting they're different."

"Stupid defiance, is all that is," Tina says, making a face like she's about to spit.

"Yes, it can seem like that. But sometimes, when we're young, we're not running toward something. We're just running away from what we don't want."

"What's there to fear? Jemell would be lucky to do as well as I've done," argues Ricky.

"That's how you see it, but I suspect Jemell would like to experiment with some other identities before foreclosing on any one in particular. Unfortunately, that's why packing delinquents together in jails so seldom prevents children from becoming worse criminals. I'm all for real, immediate consequences for kids who break the law, but jails that are there only to punish kids at best are a waste of money and at worst actually increase crime. In fact, the countries with the lowest rates of incarceration for delinquents actually have the lowest rates of recidivism and youth crime overall."

Ricky says, "So house arrest for my son Jemell is a good thing, then. It keeps him away from other bad kids who might convince him that all he can be is a damn delinquent."

"Kids have shown me that they will change when the substitutions we give them provide them with a different, but very powerful, identity. They can't find that in jail unless there are opportunities while incarcerated to become someone different. Your kids aren't in jail, but I believe they are just as desperate to find ways to describe themselves other than as problem children."

"Like what?" asks Frank.

"Like Sadie finding out that she's a young woman who is an amazing musician, DJ, fashionista, model, math whiz, sports star, or maybe — just maybe — a kid who gets the respect of her peers for giving up her dangerous lifestyle. In other words, Sadie could also be the girl who tells the other girls that she thinks having babies young is not cool."

"I like the sound of that," says Merlinda, patting Frank's knee. "We really haven't been giving Sadie a way to feel grown-up, have we? And now she's chosen a really dangerous way to convince us she's a young woman, not a child." Merlinda looks hesitantly at Frank.

"What she means is that *I* haven't exactly been seeing my daughter as a young woman who can make decisions for herself. I overprotect. But Sadie doesn't inspire confidence, either."

"We're in the same chicken-and-egg problem with Jemell," says Ricky. "I never know how much responsibility to give him. I figure he'll blow it even before I give it."

"And none of us did the same?" I tease. Frank frowns, not appreciating the joke.

"You have kids," Frank says, leaning forward, his voice testy. "Are they doing drugs? Drinking? Having sex? You never tell us about your kids. Does any of this stuff you're telling us *really* work?"

I hesitate a moment. Lots of years of training are telling me not to do what I'm about to do. I can feel myself being pulled down the vortex counsellors avoid. I'm about to talk about myself.

"Well?" Frank says, challenging me to speak. Everyone is waiting.

I try to manoeuvre my way out of this. "I know you're looking for answers, but every family is different."

"No, no, no! I want to know if this works. Do your kids develop powerful identities without drugs? Or tattoos or other crap like that?"

Slowly, I leap as if from a plane, letting the gravity of what I'm doing liberate me.

"Yes," I tell Frank, "these ideas do work for my children, too." He leans back.

"How?" asks Katherine.

"My son, Scott, is a really outgoing kind of kid. You know, very popular. I remember him really scaring me, though, when I went to pick him up one night around midnight. He'd just turned fourteen. When I arrived at the door of the house where he was, there were at least forty kids running up and down the stairs, bottles of rum and beer in their hands. And the house stank of pot. I couldn't believe the parents had left the kids unsupervised. Thankfully, my son didn't look high or drunk when he came out. On the drive home, he said it had been a crazy party, so I asked him if he had drunk anything or smoked any weed. I explained I wouldn't be upset if he had, but I just wanted to talk to him about how to keep himself safe. He said he'd had a few sips of beer, that's all. Then we talked about what he saw. He told me a remarkable thing. He said, 'It was like the whole point of the party was to get completely drunk or stoned. That's all anyone wanted to do.'"

"And what if he had drunk more or used drugs? What would you have done then?" Frank asks. I'm sure the same question is on everyone's mind.

"Oh, that happened later. But you see, what I'd learned from families like yours was that I needed to show him he could talk to me. I was embarrassed and the conversation was awkward, but at least he and I talked about what he liked about the party and what he didn't like. I didn't shut him down or lecture him. I wanted to know who he thought was a superstar and who just looked like a drunken, stoned ass. Most kids I've met are happy to tell me what they like and don't like about their delinquent friends. Even little kids will tell you, if you ask, what they like about the school bully and what they don't like. Let's face it, even bullies and teenaged stoners can look pretty cool."

"So what did you do? Forbid your son from going to those parties, I hope."

"No. That would have just said no, when what I had to figure out was how to say yes. We started talking about how he could stay safe at parties like those. If he did drink, how much would he drink? If he wanted to try pot, then how would he do it safely? I sure as hell wasn't going to buy him alcohol or dope, so these were problems he would have to solve. And I very emphatically told him I would prefer he waited until he could drink legally and that he shouldn't ever smoke weed. But I also knew that I was risking our relationship if I told him he absolutely couldn't do these things or go to those parties. I knew well enough that he would just end up lying to me! Which, by the way, is what I did with my parents."

"I know about lying," says Frank, his arms folded loosely across his chest. "I lied to my folks, too. It's sort of stupid, but I never thought my own kid would lie to me. Not all the time like Sadie does."

"My problem was I still needed to help my son find something he could say about himself at these parties that wasn't 'Hey, look at me, I'm a big stoner just like you!' Fortunately, my son is also a DJ. A year or so ago, he got interested in mixing music. We helped him rent some decks from a music store. I figured it was just a phase, a silly interest, but he's wound up getting himself hired out for house parties and school dances. Now when he goes to house parties, he has a way to be the coolest kid there that doesn't involve getting so wasted he ends up throwing up in people's cars. He's there at the front of the room, shaping the party's groove. That's status."

"I get it," says Tina. "And I'm guessing he has all that expensive equipment to watch over, so he can't get completely drunk."

"You've got it. My son has found a way to be the centre of attention at a party and not have to drink or do drugs. Not that he hasn't still made that mistake. There was at least one night when he was fifteen that I heard someone throwing up in the downstairs bathroom next to his bedroom. He had three friends sleeping over and I guessed that one of them had been too drunk to go home and confront his parents. I remember thinking my son had better clean that bathroom tomorrow because I sure as hell wasn't going to do it.

"The next morning when I went to check on the boys, it was my son who was writhing in pain on his bed, looking like hell. 'I think I've got food poisoning,' he said. 'What did you eat?' I asked, concerned, though wondering why the other three fellows were still blissfully asleep. 'Pizza and some nachos,' he said. 'Not likely to poison you, especially if no one else got sick,' I answered. Then I asked him, 'What about drinks? What did you drink?' He moaned a little, then told me, 'Just two small shots of something clear. Maybe vodka?' I couldn't help it. I laughed. I also doubted that it had been two small shots. But a bad twenty-four-hour hangover that included vomiting and diarrhea seemed like a natural enough consequence. I just shook my head each time I came to check on him. Told him, 'You'll have to clean up the bathroom when you're feeling better,' and offered to get him whatever he needed to help him feel better."

By the time I finish my story, the group is nodding their approval.

"That's helpful," says Katherine. "I see what you mean now. I have to help Amanda find something good to say about herself or else she'll go looking for that something in all the wrong places."

"That's right, Katherine. Of course, it doesn't work perfectly, but it sure helps our kids find a positive identity for themselves when we coach them on where to look."

Before we wrap up for the evening, I invite everyone to talk about their own experiments with different identities. How, when, and where did they find some way of proudly proclaiming themselves to the world?

I then ask them to do a little homework: stealth observation of their child. While I don't want them snooping in their child's personal spaces, like computers or drawers, I encourage them to look at what's on the walls of their child's room. Who are their child's friends? What are some of their child's habits? Who is this emerging young person who is like each of her parents, and yet so different, too?

"If you can, tell me next week what you find out."

Then, as I've done every other evening, I pass out a cue card.

Things Our Children Need
5. A Powerful Identity

- As parents, we are mirrors for our children. We reflect back to them who they are and how much they are valued.
- Our children's identities are theirs to choose, as long as they don't do long-term harm to themselves or others.
- As parents, we can offer children substitute identities that are just as powerful as the troubling identities they may tumble into.

Before the group ends, Frank says, "Thank you." We both know what he means. It's not what I said tonight, but what I did. I brought myself more fully into the group.

"You're welcome," I say. I'm still worried I might have set the bar too high. If my kids succeed, then are other parents failures if their kids don't do as well as mine? I know that's not true. Parenting is not a very predictable enterprise, no matter how good we are. Much of what we do is art, our children the constantly transforming canvas on which we paint.

Chapter 11

The Sixth Thing Children Need — A Sense of Control

When I was ten, my father accepted a job managing a clothing manufac-turer in a small town two hundred miles west of Montreal, and we moved. Rather than commute on raised highways, he now travelled eight miles down quiet roads to an industrial park where the factory had been built.

My school went from 465 students to less than a hundred. I also skipped a grade. Not only was I now the new kid, I was also brainy, which in that school meant I was horribly out of place. The other kids couldn't understand why I read so much. Or why I laughed in English class when the teacher asked for the plural of *you*, and the boy next to me said "youse." The more I laughed, the more confused everyone looked, except for the teacher. She looked constipated, like she wanted to say something but feared for her life if she did.

I couldn't have cared less about school. What mattered most to me was that at home, my father seemed happier than ever before. We had a two-storey house and I had my own bedroom. We owned a pickup truck and my father had installed a CB radio and an eight-foot antenna that waved in the wind at the back of the truck like some sinister James Bond spy gadget. We each got our own handles so we could call one another. I was Chocolate Bear and my father was Bagel Man. Weekends we spent washing the truck or installing yet another piece of audio equipment.

Soon my older brother bought himself a 70cc dirt bike that I would take out into the countryside by myself for hours, tracing my way down logging roads that ringed the small town where we'd settled. I got my own motorcycle the next year, a twenty-year-old Indian Airplane, a heavy behemoth of a bike with a 100cc engine.

My mother put in a garden and spent her days shopping.

Each summer, I went to work with my father for a few weeks. He arranged for my brother and me to help do inventory at the factory. Though it meant being indoors, the money was great and I enjoyed climbing high up onto piles of boxes of imported goods from India and calling out identification codes and quantities to the regular employees, who kept tallies of the goods.

For a brief moment, life felt normal. At home, we even had a picket fence surrounding our backyard, where an above-ground pool endlessly perplexed my father with its gurgling, air blocks, algae, and leaks. I don't remember him falling asleep in his La-Z-Boy like he used to do in Montreal. Instead, I remember him volunteering to help find a lost child, he and his invisible friends coordinating their search through their CBs.

It made no sense to me why he was so happy when he got a call from his former employer back in the city. I overhead him talking to my mother at the kitchen table. Words like *raise* and *vice-president* thundered the loudest. Afterward my mother looked like she'd been crying. And then my motorcycle caught fire. I didn't mean to destroy it. While changing the battery, I'd accidentally crossed wires and somehow the innards of the machine ignited. I ran for the hose, thinking water would help. By the time my brother arrived and threw an old car blanket over the steaming mess, there wasn't much left to salvage.

We moved back to the city a few months later. We kept the truck for a year, but it was too expensive to run and my parents traded it for a Dodge Colt, a gutless tin box with plastic seats and no CB. I focused entirely on my life at school. I became the editor of the school newspaper and won the lead in the school play. My father disappeared from my life, his commute starting at 6:00 a.m. I wouldn't see him until he returned at 6:00 p.m. and then only briefly. He'd come in quietly, sit, and eat dinner alone, with my mother hovering near the kitchen table, guarding him from interruptions from us kids.

I can't remember if he came to see the play. By then, it didn't matter so much.

The Friday after our group meeting, I volunteer to help my son DJ a junior high dance. I work as his roadie, lugging gear, helping to connect speakers, and setting up lights. I wear a faded black T-shirt and old jeans. I put a tattered ball cap on my head. My son spins the tunes, explaining to me how he paces the crowd. Some songs build the rhythm, others slow it down. He can actually adjust the speed at which songs are played to build the intensity. He uses a $2,000 MacBook Pro to mix music. He paid for half of it himself; the rest was my gift. The computer is attached to a Sorretto box that helps create the magic of the mixes.

The gym is lit with spinning LEDs and a disco ball. Lasers streak the walls and floor. The speakers are set extra heavy on the bass. The school's head girl comes over with a playlist: "Each class got to choose ten songs." My son has at least a hundred thousand tunes on his computer. He'll play the clean versions of the requests, though the kids pressure him to play the versions from their iPods. He looks at the teachers standing, arms crossed, at the far wall and explains he can't do that.

I spend most of the evening flanking his right side, letting him know when one of the kids wants to request a song or helping him adjust the speakers as the room becomes more crowded and the ambient noise rises. The kids pack together in tight mosh pits, the girls much closer than the boys at first. Then, as there is more anonymity on the floor, couples pair off. All night, groups of boys and girls scream onto the dance floor and off again, voting with their feet for their likes and dislikes. In the shadowy corners, girls and boys huddle, arms linked over shoulders, shouting lyrics at the ceiling.

Girls head to the bathroom in packs. Boys go in small bands of twos and threes, only to be followed by armed police officers who have been hired to be there. After an hour I have to put in my earplugs or risk going deaf.

From time to time, there are spontaneous explosions of dance. One boy does a backflip, then a one-handed handstand and shoulder twirl. The crowd gives him space and my son adjusts the music. The other boys play their part, gently pushing the dancer back into the middle of their circle when he tries to leave. This friendly mime all part of the energy, testosterone running free. Another tune is played and the spell is broken. That's when I see Sadie.

She's wearing a short green dress. Strapless. It's pulled very tight, making the most of her early development. She is bent slightly over and a young man in a white shirt and sagging jeans is behind her, his crotch rhythmically grinding into her. Her hands are on her knees and she lets him sway her side to side, until he grabs her across the chest and lifts her and swings her in a circle. She smiles coyly, then lands as her partner disappears into the crowd. She barely seems to notice, raises her hands above her head, and begins pulling magical strands of invisible rope as if ringing heavenly bells. Three girls surround her and she is swallowed back into the crowd.

I pull my ball cap lower across my eyes, fearing she'll see me. But I'm behind the lights. An impossible presence. I belong in an office, not here. I suspect she could look me in the face and not know me.

The dance is over by 10:00 p.m. Everyone leaves and the police secure the bathrooms while we disassemble the equipment. The gym looks stark and lifeless without the kids and the party lights.

"So what did you think?" my son asks as I'm coiling cables.

"Fascinating," is the best I can manage right then. "Just fascinating."

He grins, like he's talking to a small child. He's enjoyed showing me what he does. "You can roadie for me anytime," he teases. For a moment, I shiver with the warmth of our connection.

On the way out to my car, arms full of computer equipment, I notice that many of the kids have gathered in the parking lot next to the school. Lines of sweaty boys and girls, one wearing a green dress. I can't see Sadie's face. She's bent over, throwing up beside a tree. Two girls stand over her, rubbing her back. For a second I think about stopping to help but know that she'd be embarrassed and worried I'd tell her parents. Still, I stop and watch from across the street, making sure that she's okay. Sadie stands up, wobbling from side to side. Then she's put into the back seat of one of the boys' cars. Her friends, giggling, slide in beside her. The young man who's driving guns his engine. He has a new Mustang. I shake my head but can do nothing at that moment except watch and hope Sadie is safe.

The next morning I call Merlinda. "I was wondering if I could get a time to meet with Sadie and both you and Frank?" I try to sound nonchalant. "I haven't seen her in a long time and was wondering how the parenting strategies from the course are working."

"Yes, that would be good. She's not here now. She stayed last night at a friend's after a school dance. She had our permission this time. It's nice to see her hanging out with some nice young people for once."

I smack my forehead with my fist. "Yes, that's good," I say. "But can we meet early next week? Maybe Monday?" Our next evening meeting is scheduled for Wednesday.

"Frank is going to be away but I can come in with Sadie. Is there a reason for the rush?"

I'm not sure what to say but decide not to ruin Merlinda's weekend. "No," I lie and leave it at that.

Sadie says, "I guess we're like our own little group — the outsiders. That's who I want my friends to be. It's like the kids look at us, with all our black makeup and our music, and they think we're vampires or witches. What's wrong with that?"

"Everything," shouts Merlinda. I'm just as surprised as Sadie by Merlinda's raised voice. "You've ruined your hair. You were such a cute little brunette. But this black, inky mess you've made of yourself. It's not pretty."

"Yeah. Cute, little. I'm tired of being like that. You and Dad don't want me to grow up, do you? Tell the truth. You really don't, do you?"

"Not like this. And besides, you've only just turned thirteen. You're still my baby girl."

"Oh, that's perfect," Sadie says and rolls her eyes. She does it perfectly. A big round orbit that eclipses her blue irises. I'm enjoying the performance, but I have to stop this mother-daughter joust before Sadie decides to march out of my office. She might frighten my co-workers if she did. She's no longer dressed as the party girl from the week before. Today she's a raging, dark sorceress with the wrath of the undead in search of blood, straight out of *Twilight*.

"Okay, so that isn't how you want to be seen, is it?" I say.

"No shit." Sadie thrusts her tiny legs, firm as tent pegs, into the floor in front of her. "I just like being with the Emos. They're my friends."

"Emos?" I ask.

"The kids with the black trench coats. Just because they're dressed different doesn't mean they're bad kids. Honestly, my parents were once just as outrageous. I've seen their prom photos, with their crazy haircuts."

Merlinda grimaces. "Yes, but that doesn't mean you have to be so different, does it?"

"Oh, for God's sake. We're just kids having fun. The other kids think we're witches, the dorks. I can make like I'm casting a spell, like we read in *Macbeth*, and they all go freaky!"

"You could have a lot of fun with this, couldn't you?" I say, trying to put Sadie at ease. For Merlinda, who sits up straighter, keeping herself composed, this sounds like heresy.

"Mostly we just stand alone by ourselves at the corner of the cafeteria. No one is hitting on me or anything. At least not in my group. I've only been asked out on a date once, and that was by this preppy guy. I think he was just looking for a cheap excuse for a girlfriend."

"I don't understand," says Merlinda. "Why would *you* be cheap?"

"He thinks I'd be easy, that's all. But he's just stupid. All those boys are stupid," Sadie says and slouches a little, her hands deep in her pockets, her face turned away. Her posture confuses me. The last time we met, she was happy to growl at us and make like sex was nothing.

I say, "You have a right to be different, Sadie." She nods. Merlinda stares at me, waiting for me to make Sadie tell us what's really going on. I don't think I could make her talk even if I tried. Instead, I say, "Being more responsible for yourself comes with the responsibility to keep yourself safe and to reassure your parents you're making good decisions."

"Whatever," says Sadie, slouching further down in her seat.

Merlinda hesitates, then asks me, "So you're saying if Sadie wants to be older, she can be, but she has to act like an adult, too. Not a little kid." Merlinda is slowly understanding what I'm doing.

"What about you, Sadie? Willing to move into adulthood? Sounds like your mom might be willing to give you fewer rules if you can prove you can act responsibly."

"I doubt it."

"She let you go to the dance last week. And stay out overnight."

"It took me forever to convince her. And when I came home, all she did was tell me how tired I looked and how worried she'd been." Merlinda is about to jump in, but I reach out my hand, a gesture she understands to mean *wait*.

Looking straight at Sadie, then at Merlinda, and finally back at Sadie, I ask her tenderly, "What would you have liked your mom to have said?"

Sadie squints her eyes and pulls her mouth tight. She looks like she's about to cry. "She never asked me if I had any fun ... or ... if the other kids liked my dress ... or anything...." She's upset and her words choke on tears that she lets out in a single stream down her left cheek. She takes a tissue from the box next to her and blows her nose loudly, like a child would do.

"I did ask those things. You never listened."

"No, you didn't. You're just trying to make yourself look good in front of Michael," Sadie yells.

I jump in, as much to help Merlinda save face as to calm Sadie down. "I'm not sure what you said or didn't say, Merlinda, but it sounds like Sadie wants you in her life. That's what I just heard her say. Only she doesn't want you and Frank treating her like a little kid. She wants some control, too."

I must have hit the mark because Sadie stops shouting.

Now the difficult work begins. Merlinda will need to find a way to be in her daughter's life but still set limits that don't threaten Sadie's emerging need for more control over the parts of her life she's ready to handle. The trouble, though, with any strategy that tries to get Sadie more autonomy is that her parents have to trust her, and they won't trust her if she looks like she has risen from the crypt or doesn't come home when she should. Those are problems I can't solve right away but at least we're getting closer to untangling this parent-child relationship.

"Sadie, I think your parents are ready to give you more control. But I'm a little worried. As I'm sure your mother and father are, too. You've been breaking curfew. And your friends are older than you. With more freedom. That's not something most young people your age have. Everyone is worried about you getting into a dangerous situation. Maybe in a car with someone you don't know. Or maybe being asked to drink or do drugs."

If looks could vaporize, Sadie's would destroy me. She doesn't know how I know, but she can see I know a lot more than I should. Her eyes flit from my face, sideways to her mother's, and then back to me. Anger changes to a silent plea: *Don't!* I keep staring right at her. "I won't betray you," I want to tell her. But I also won't let her recklessly endanger herself, either.

"Yes, we're very worried about those things," says Merlinda, unaware of what just happened. "Not that she's done anything like that yet. Right, honey?"

Sadie shrugs. She can't outright lie in front of me.

"Is there anything you want to tell your mom? Can you reassure her you're making good decisions for yourself?"

"I am!"

"It's just that, no matter who you're with, if they're older, they'll be making decisions that might put you in harm's way. I think we all know there are possibilities to drink or do drugs. And if you're getting into cars with strangers, there is the possibility you end up unintentionally in some dangerous situations. Physically, sexually."

"I know!" Sadie yells, her hands now gripping the arms of her chair as if she's ready to bolt from the room. That's my cue to slow down.

"Okay, I know you do. I just wanted to be sure your mom knows that you are thinking about these things. The safer you keep yourself, the more you show yourself to be mature and strong. If you do that, I think your parents are going to give you more freedom. That's what you want, right?"

"Yes," she answers, sounding frustrated, her voice breaking. "Except they're not doing that. They make it like I have to ..." She doesn't finish her sentence.

"To what, Sadie?" Merlinda asks.

"Oh, never mind."

"To lie?" I say as quietly as I can and still be heard. I lean forward, inviting Sadie with my gaze to tell her mother what she's really doing.

Sadie turns her head toward the wall and begins to cry. Merlinda is confused. "I got into someone's car after the dance last week and we all went to this guy's place where we were drinking. But we got back to Jinny's all right. I was never in any danger." Sadie looks at her mother, who has her hands up in front of her mouth, gasping.

"That took courage," I say and wait a moment for Merlinda to calm. Then I ask Sadie, "I know this might sound like a strange question, but can you tell us what you *liked* about getting in the car? The drinking?"

She looks at me for a moment, suspicious that I'm laying a trap for her. But my voice sounds earnest. "All of it. No one looked at me like I could be carried away. I could make my own decisions. I got home okay, didn't I?"

"This time. But what about next time? Do you do this often?" asks Merlinda, her brow drenched with fear.

"Jeez, Mom, like, no. You don't let me out enough to do it ever. Except this once. I had to lie. You made me lie!"

"Oh, Sadie, I don't want you to lie. Your father doesn't want you to lie. If you really need something, tell us. We'll take you where you want to go. I had no idea you were really ready for all these grown-up things. I just don't want you to get hurt." And then it's Merlinda's turn to cry, and then Sadie cries some more, and I want to give Merlinda an A-plus for parenting with compassion. That was beautiful. Maybe not a cure for everything that ails their relationship, but an eloquent attempt to build a bridge.

"We all want control of our lives," I tell the group at our next regular meeting. "We adults are no different than our kids. We want to know that we have the power to influence what happens to us. That we have some say over how people treat us, love us, and to whom we return that love. We also want control over the small things in life, too. The four-year-old wants to decide what pajamas he wears to bed. The fourteen-year-old wants to decide when he goes to bed. And the twenty-four-year-old wants to decide whether that bed is in his own apartment or back home with his parents." I've got the group's attention. Frank seems more relaxed tonight. Merlinda sits next to him, her hand resting on his knee. I was worried Frank might not come back. When change doesn't happen quickly, people sometimes fire me.

"Sadie, Jemell, Amanda, all want control. But it's up to us to give it to them in manageable amounts."

"Sadie doesn't much like waiting, if you know what I mean," Merlinda tells the group.

"The trick," I explain, "is to let our kids have enough control that they learn the consequences of their actions, but not so much control that the consequences will be beyond their capacity to cope."

"I'm not sure I'm following you," says Tina. "Jemell wants to be a full-fledged adult. Now. Not tomorrow."

"Yes, I understand that. But that's a formula for disaster. I think control and consequences go together. Or as a Supreme Court judge I know likes to say, 'If you do the crime, then you'd better be prepared to do the time.' In other words, if our kids are old enough to insist we let them screw up, 'Fine,' I say, 'but first reassure me that you can handle the consequences.' If my child wants to stay up late and he's just eight years old, then he has to convince me he can get up in the morning, get ready for school, and stay awake at his desk. When he's responsible enough to do all that, he gets some say over his bedtime. Notice I said 'some say.' I still hold the veto on all decisions concerning bedtimes."

"I like that," says Katherine. "Amanda prefers to hear me say yes to her, but sometimes, honestly, she's completely naive about the consequences of her actions. What do I do then?"

"That's where the structure we provide comes in. I'm not saying abdicate your crown! You are still the family ruler. But your princes and princesses need to test their abilities to be sovereign beings, too. Say yes to what you can say yes to. Rather than saying no to what your kids can't do, try saying, 'When you are older, we can talk about this again.'"

"But what if I don't like Amanda's choices? You know, like not doing her homework. Don't I help her to see that she's making a mistake?"

"I know this is going to be difficult to hear, but sometimes, when a child is bound and determined to make a decision on her own — like not doing her homework — we may have to let her make a *bad* decision and then help her deal with the consequences. Of course, I would prefer children accept the sage counsel of their parents, but sometimes our kids checkmate us. When it comes to homework, for example, we can tell a child she will lose all her screen time unless she gets her work done, but there is nothing we can do to force children to get good grades or value learning.

"I like the way New Orleans poet Andrei Codrescu talks about such independence. In a city full of eccentrics, he says 'True misfits don't need help.' He's got a point. When a kid doesn't see herself as part of the get-an-education-get-a-job-get-a-mortgage-have-a-baby-and-settle-down culture, there's no amount of convincing that is going to get that kid to fit with others' expectations of her."

I can see the parents are disappointed. They must have thought I was going to grant their wish and make their kids into responsible little beings overnight. Maybe it's my fear of conformity, but I don't want kids to just fit in. I want them to experience their lives as fully as possible and suffer the consequences, good and bad. I like children who resist conformity, though I will still insist they meet minimum expectations like learning how to read and do basic math.

It's like the elderly man who, against everyone's advice, drives himself to his doctor's appointment. His wife calls him on his cellphone to tell him she's been listening to the news and has heard that a car is headed in the wrong direction on the interstate highway. "Be careful!" she shouts at him. "Someone's driving the wrong way."

"What do you mean, some*one*!" he shouts back. "They're *all* driving the wrong way."

Our kids are no different and are just as self-assured. Our job as their parents isn't to just tell them which way to head. It's to teach them how to take control of their own lives and then to be there when they screw up and need our help to fix the mess they've made.

"That's awfully hard to do," says Tina. On that point, we can all agree.

To show everyone what I mean, I tell them about Paula, a six-year-old girl with uncombed hair and mismatched socks who was caught stealing candy from a corner store next to her school playground. She had been pilfering gummy worms and sour tarts for weeks before anyone noticed. All the candy she stole she gave to other children who were, of course, much more willing afterward to include her when they played skipping games or chased each other through the imaginary alligator pit that was beneath their monkey bars.

Except for stealing candy, there isn't very much else that Paula would say is special about herself. Her hair isn't shiny and extra long like her friend Lara's. She isn't athletic like Patti. And she seldom understands what her teachers are teaching, unlike her neighbour Farah whose parents make her study with a tutor after school every day. Paula's parents are too busy coping with a mortgage that is about to be foreclosed to keep track of Paula's problems at school. Paula has known all year that her family is different from others, where mothers and fathers pack lovely lunches for their children and seem to have lots of time to read to them.

As a family therapist, I was expected to fix Paula. I decided instead to let Paula be my teacher. "What can you do that no one else can do?" I asked the embarrassed little girl who came to see me with her mother.

Paula shrugged and said, "I don't know."

"Honestly, is there something you can do well that the other kids can't do?"

"You mean like stealing candy?" Paula said hesitantly.

Paula was right. Stealing candy was something she could do very well. From her point of view, she had found a perfectly reasonable solution to the problem of being alone on the playground or feeling stupid in class. All on her own, she'd managed to make the other children like her.

It takes a special set of glasses to see Paula this way. Instead of rejecting her, I needed to appreciate her need to control her life and the wacky way she had done it.

But how can I, as a parent, love a child with problems? I don't want to live with a thief. I don't want to cuddle on my knee a foul-mouthed delinquent. I don't want to go to a movie with a child who, when I look at him, all I see is defiance or a pothead, a dropout, a brat, or a misfit. What I need to see, just as Paula helped me see, is the other 90 percent of any child that is mostly problem free. The child who likes to have friends. The child who appreciates a good laugh. The child who is clever in a mischievous way.

Learning from Paula, it was easy to help her stop stealing. I just had to find her something else that she could do just as well. Turns out Paula could help teach preschoolers their colours and even their numbers. Her teachers gave her permission to spend an hour twice a week helping in the pre-kindergarten attached to her elementary school. On the playground, one of Paula's teachers asked Patti to show Paula how to play the games the girls liked to play. And at home, it took no time at all to gently remind Paula's parents that their daughter needed a bit more of their time. We decided to forget about disciplining Paula and worked instead on finding her *substitutes* for her problem behaviour that were meaningful to her and that she felt she controlled.

Katherine raises her hand, then remembers she can speak anytime she likes. "I don't think children are the only ones who mess up, you know. I think my Amanda has had to live with a lot of my mistakes, too." The other parents look embarrassed but seem to know Katherine is speaking for all of us. Troubled kids aren't born. To some degree, they are raised.

Jeannette Walls, in her memoir, *The Glass Castle*, shows us just how awful parents can be when they give children far too much control. Burned while cooking herself a hot dog at age four, Walls tells us how her father stole her away from her hospital bed before her burns had healed, likely to save money on medical bills. The little girl's early life was a long procession of hotel rooms and trailers where her parents stayed until they couldn't pay the rent, then skedaddled. The worst part, Walls remembers, is that even if they were starving, the children were told to pretend they were on an adventure. That adventure included being thrown from a moving car, and physical abuse and neglect at the hands of selfish narcissists who were plagued by alcoholism and mental illness. It's an extreme example of how badly we can parent, but it makes a point. A child without some say over her life is going to be a child who is vulnerable to the bad decisions of others.

Unfortunately, we are trapped under the influence of a historical Darwinism that makes us think of children as lesser-evolved beings, like puppies. Where adults are fully human, children are thought of as impulsive beasts that should be caged.

I tell everyone, "Think back to when you were a little kid." They hesitate, then slowly, one by one, relax into their memories. "How did your parents make you feel like powerful people who could tackle your own problems? Did they make you feel you mattered? That you were strong and capable?"

There are very few among us who will say they appreciated feeling powerless while growing up. Or who will smile and say, "Oh, I wish my parents had shipped me off to a boot camp and let people yell at me all day." More likely, we wanted a parent who convinced us that we could make responsible decisions, and that they would be there for us when we made mistakes.

I explain, "Control depends on both. I meet a lot of very scared children who have too little structure or caring, who are left with responsibilities rivalling those of Jeannette Walls. To develop well, a child needs to be able to say, this is what I can influence, and this is beyond my influence. It's a question of what's called *attribution*. We risk becoming depressed if we attribute our success to things we can't control (like what our parents did rather than what we did ourselves) and our failures to things we can. In fact, a good parent will help a child feel more in control of those things she can reasonably expect to change."

Ricky looks at Tina, then Frank, and whistles softly.

"I'm not convincing you, am I?"

Ricky shakes his head. "I don't mean to be rude, but control? Control! That is the last thing Jemell needs. Seems kids these days have far too much of that already."

"Yes. I can see how it might seem like that. Jemell has pushed you and Tina every step of the way."

"He controls everything. He bosses around his siblings, bullies us for money. It's like some crown prince is living with us, with his big attitude. I liked what you said about structure and discipline, but this stuff about control smells like dog crap."

"To be honest, I'm often plagued with very similar doubts. We provide our kids structure, consequences, and connections. All of that provides the perfect environment for them to develop their full potential. Except what I'm talking about now is the skills they need to take full advantage of the safe and predictable worlds we provide them. We've already said they need to explore relationships if they are going to become fully functioning adults. What I'm saying tonight is that they also need the chance to learn how to control the world around them. But we have to *teach* them how to do that properly."

"And how do we do that?" asks Ricky.

"The best way I know to answer that question is to tell you another story. This one about a boy named Alex."

Alex is one of those kids who oozes potential but keeps disappointing. The eldest son of two hard-working parents, Alex played AAA hockey until his coach demoted him to AA when he kept coming late to practices. Alex was good enough that the AA coach wanted him to be the captain, but Alex said no. He said it involved too much responsibility. I think he was embarrassed to have been put down a level. It wasn't long before he was late for most of those practices, too, and was being told to either shape up or he'd be off the team.

His parents didn't understand. Alex's father was a selfmade man with a successful truck repair business that he and his wife had started after they emigrated from South Africa. They'd left practically everything they owned behind, packed themselves and their three kids onto a boat, and arrived in North America with little more than dreams of finding a place where there was less violence and more equality. Alex's mother eventually found work as a bookkeeper in the municipal office of the small town where the family lives. Alex's parents are proud people who will tell you what they think —and what they think Alex needs to change — without hesitation.

As lazy and unmotivated as Alex was at the ice arena, he was just as much of a problem at home. If his little brother made lunch, Alex took it for himself. If his twin sister was watching her favourite show, and Alex wanted to watch cage wrestling, he grabbed the remote and changed the channel. No amount of screaming got him to turn the channel back. If his sister dug her nails into his arm, crying and protesting, he pulled her hair or kicked her until she stopped. Alex's parents worked too many hours to supervise the children all the time. Most evenings it felt like they entered a war zone, with battle-weary children encamped on one side of the house and Alex sprawled on the sofa, ignoring his chores and homework.

It was the homework that was particularly troubling to Alex's parents. Alex was likely to fail grade eleven. He shrugged when his parents reminded him of the consequences. School and Alex have always been like oil and water. They just don't mix. Alex hates it that he struggles academically. He is supposed to take medication to help him cope with his attention deficit disorder, but he doesn't like the way the medicine calms him. Instead, he likes to impress the smart girls who think he's someone special outside the classroom. Or at least they did until he lost his spot on the AAA hockey team.

If Alex seemed nonchalant about his life, it's because he said nothing much matters. He got money from his parents when he needed it. If he didn't do his chores, someone else would do them for him. A cleaning lady did most of the housework, anyway. None of the children had dinner-making responsibilities. It's a life in which Alex existed as a child in a grown-up's body. He had the power to make his own decisions and no responsibility for the consequences. The only thing that anyone was certain worried Alex was that his friends would go into grade twelve and he'd be left behind if he failed. That might have motivated him to, as his father would say, get "dirty with studying," except Alex figured he could drop out and be with his friends during their free periods.

"Really," he told me during one of our meetings together, "what's the problem?"

I surprised Alex and his parents when I suggested that rather than telling Alex no, we find ways to invite him to take *more* control of his life in ways appropriate for a fifteen-year-old. We started with Alex's bullying of his siblings. Alex was given a choice: either find a way to compromise or watch television separately from the rest of the family. A week later, Alex still hadn't figured out what *compromise* meant, so his parents put some structure in place that would separate Alex. Alex was given an old television for his room. If he wanted to watch the big-screen LED in the living room, he would have to wait until his parents were home.

"And what if I decide to watch the big screen, anyway?" he threatened. His parents looked nervously over at me. They hadn't a clue what they could do to enforce the rule.

"I have a few ideas," I said. "Alex, if you are old enough to disobey your parents and make your own decisions, then you are also old enough to have much more responsibility for yourself. If you don't remain apart from your siblings and watch your own television, then your parents will have to cut off the cable service to your room. They pay for that service each month. A young man who is old enough to make his own decisions is likely old enough to pay his own cable bill."

Alex smiled. He was sure his parents wouldn't seriously consider doing anything so mean to him. When they cut his cable a week later, Alex ended up back on the couch again, with his sister in tears. That's when his parents hired a babysitter. A university student living next door was asked to come in three afternoons a week. Her job was to help the children with their homework and to see to it that Alex stayed away from the big-screen television. A set of rules, posted on Alex's door, made it very clear what was expected of him. Alex's parents offered to help their son find work, if he liked, to pay for his own cable. Maybe even to buy his own LED television.

Alex was furious and embarrassed, especially when his friends heard there was a babysitter looking after him. But the solution worked. Rather than taking Alex's power away, his parents had strategically manoeuvred around their son and invited him to take more control of his own life. They had made sure he understood that the natural consequence of fighting with his siblings was separation, then supervision. They also, through their actions more than their words, told their son they expected him to take some control of his life. That included getting a job.

What they were doing began to help. Alex didn't like being banished to his room to watch television, nor did he like the thought of having to earn his own money. It was only a week later that he agreed to negotiate with his siblings the use of the television. He even showed some maturity when he suggested they decide in advance each week which shows each child could watch.

That still, however, left Alex with the serious problem of failing grades. Here again, the solution was to invite Alex to take more control of his life. As Alex would soon be without an education and likely needing to support himself, his parents thought it time he began to understand what it means to work at a low-paying job for long hours. They insisted Alex get a job at a local fast-food restaurant. They would no longer give him an allowance. In exchange, they told their son, he could look after his own studies. They would no longer nag at him to do his homework.

"If he was old enough to work, then he was too old for us to be telling him what to do about school," his mother said.

Alex failed his year.

"What!" shouts Frank. "You let him fail?"

"I'm not sure I let him do anything," I answer in my own defence.

"So let me see if I got this," says Tina. "You fixed the fighting between Alex and his sister by giving him control over his own television and insisting he act like an adult if he was going to be in the same room as his sister and brother."

"Correct."

"And you had the parents not give him any more money, because

Alex needed to learn what it would be like to fail at school and work at a low-paying job."

"Correct again. We all wanted Alex to take control of his life —"

"Wait, I'm not done. But you also let Alex lose his school year? I'm with Frank on this. That sounds crazy."

"But Alex made that choice," I say. "It was something he could reasonably change if he had wanted to." I pause for a moment to let my words settle. "Now, please, in fairness, I always believed Alex would eventually do the right thing and finish his studies. And Alex was likely going to fail his year, anyway. Remember, no amount of nagging had gotten him to study. His parents had even provided him with a tutor in his own home. Still, he skipped classes, ignored assignments, and just refused to learn. At least, with him working for minimum wage, he understood the consequences. Especially when he was fired from that job for not showing up on time and missing shifts altogether."

"But," says Katherine, "if he lost that job, had no allowance, and was angry at his parents, wouldn't he just go and rob someone?"

"That's a good point. There is always a chance that things will get worse, much worse. But I think we have to ask ourselves as parents of a child like Alex, what else can we do except give a boy like this control over things he should control? We can't force a fifteen-year-old to study. But we can make him *uncomfortable* with his choices."

Katherine looks worried. Would Amanda turn to stealing if she were similarly cornered? "Remember — Alex had two parents modelling for him what it meant to pay your own way in life. And he had their support. At any time, he could have made his life better. He could have put more effort into school and hockey. He could have gotten another job. He could have acted like an adult around his home, to which his parents would quickly have responded and happily given him back his allowance and television privileges."

"So what happened?" Merlinda asks. Frank waves at me to keep going.

Alex and his parents kept sparring. Alex threatened to run away if they didn't give him money. They held their ground. When Alex stopped coming home at his curfew, they suggested he go and sleep at a friend's house. At first Alex appreciated the freedom. A few nights later, he missed his room and the quiet routine of his own family.

Against the impulse to punish their son, Alex's parents kept giving him the message that his life was his to shape. Eventually, by the time he turned sixteen and was well into his second try at grade eleven, Alex came to his parents in tears. Oddly, it was something small that finally broke him. He'd been in the cafeteria and talking to one of his friends from the year before. He told his mother how the boy had let slip that there'd been a party on the weekend, a party Alex hadn't been invited to attend. That's a dangerous moment for a kid like Alex. He could have decided enough was enough. He could have started drinking heavily or gotten wasted on drugs. He could have run away, dropped out, or even suicided. Instead, he chose to talk to his mother. Tears streaming down his face, he said he was sorry. He just didn't know what to do.

"Of course," I explain, "the amount of control a child needs is different for children of different ages. Alex was a young man. But the lessons are the same for younger children. When it comes to learning what psychologists call self-efficacy, children need experiences of control and mastery.

"A five-year-old can look after a goldfish or a plant and see that what she does or doesn't do matters. A seven-year-old can have his own library card and choose books he wants to read, can order his own food in a restaurant, and manage a small allowance on his own, including saving enough money to buy presents for his friends for birthdays and holidays. A ten-year-old can do small jobs for neighbours, like walking a dog or cleaning out a shed. She can help repair her bike tire when it goes flat and even spend an hour roaming the mall with a few friends unsupervised. A twelve-year-old can plan and cook a meal for the family. He can negotiate his own bedtime on the weekend, and within limits, choose what movie he goes to see with his friends. He can change his hair colour or wear just about anything he wants that doesn't make his parents feel too uncomfortable.

"At each stage, we want our children to feel a little more in control of their lives and better able to shape the world around them. Not only is that the foundation for genuine self-esteem, it also helps raise a child to think responsibly."

"You're sure?" asks Katherine.

"Pretty sure," I tell her with a mischievous grin.

Merlinda and Katherine exchange looks of mutual concern. I get the sense it may be time to wrap things up for the evening.

I ask for questions, and we chat amiably about how difficult it can be, as parents, to know when to control our children and when to loosen the apron strings. As time moves on, I suggest we break for the evening, then give them each a cue card.

Things Our Children Need
6. A Sense of Control

- Our children need opportunities to control their own lives and learn the consequences of their actions.
- Our children's experiences of control should match their age and ability. Children benefit little, if at all, from being burdened too young with decisions they shouldn't have to make and can't make well.
- If children abuse the control they have, the consequences they suffer should help teach them to act responsibly.
- Experiences of control give children an edge in life. They help protect children from being taken advantage of by others.
- It's good for children to attribute both their successes and failures to themselves when both are true.

After everyone has left, I turn on my computer and settle comfortably into the stillness of the evening. Before checking my email, I look out the window at the building under construction across the street. It's a hulking cement frame with bits of rebar cresting the top of each pillar like metal claws waiting for the next floor to hold in place.

I suddenly realize how tired I am. I look outside, and my mind begins to drift through memories that I've been hiding from all night.

I wasn't in much better shape than that building when I moved out to live on my own. I was just sixteen and a work in progress. The decision to leave was made the day my mother went to slap me for talking back and I held her outstretched hand in mine, staring into her frightened eyes. My father said nothing when he came home that night, but I think we both knew I had to leave.

It was shortly afterward that I found a way to start university. I had been working for years, saving money. Tuition fees were low. My parents gave me fifteen dollars a week to pay for my food. They said that's what it cost to have me at home. They didn't begrudge me the support but gave me nothing more. I worked twenty hours a week to cover my expenses. I was fully emancipated and much too young to understand the consequences.

The university courses weren't the challenge. I could even handle my dorm mates' expectations that I get wasted on massive amounts of drugs and alcohol every weekend. I knew better. I showed restraint and took some pride in controlling myself. I had to. There was no one else to look after me or pay my bills. I busied myself with evening shifts working at the campus library and spent nights at a local hotel as a front desk clerk. For once, I felt tremendously powerful with every decision my own to make and the consequences as natural and severe as an empty fridge.

My parents had practically disowned me. Or maybe I had disowned them. It didn't really matter. What mattered was the seriousness of my search for a place where I felt I belonged, and a sense of myself as someone worth loving.

Chapter 12

The Seventh Thing Children Need — A Sense of Belonging, Spirituality, and Life Purpose

At our seventh meeting, Frank tells us Sadie was raped. By this point, the Last Problem Child Group has given these families a place to come and talk openly with other parents whom they trust, especially during the worst of times.

I tell them, "Sadie will soon feel better — never the same, but better," and for a moment, we all seem a little more hopeful.

It's then that our conversation turns to spirituality and life purpose. It seems fitting that at this emotionally desperate time, we would try to remember our higher purpose as parents: to remind our children they are part of something bigger than just themselves.

I explain, "A colleague and friend, Froma Walsh, who retired after teaching family therapy at the University of Chicago, tells us that a deep inner feeling of connectedness is the basis for resilience. Whether through the organized practice of religion, or a spirituality found among friends, or even a contemplative hike through the woods, a person who holds a belief that her life has a higher purpose is likely to do better than one who drifts aimlessly without a set of values as her guide. Our children need connectedness and the moral compass that connections bring. But they also need the opportunity to give something back to others that makes it obvious to everyone the child is telling us, 'This is where I belong!'"

Katherine raises her hand tentatively. "What about kids who have no one or feel like they have no one?" she asks, unsure if it's appropriate to draw attention away from Sadie. "Or who don't have a father, like my Amanda? Can Amanda ever really feel complete without both her parents?" Katherine has stumbled upon a big question.

"There are a lot of ways that children cope," I answer. "And there are many sources of inspiration and hope, too. Melissa Elliott, a family therapist in Charlottesville, Virginia, with a national reputation for her work on spirituality, is awed by how gracefully people find ways to talk to that which cannot be seen. I've heard her tell the story of a boy who lost his mother to depression, then suicide. He was feeling very much alone and thinking about killing himself when he came to see her at her clinic. He never did attempt suicide. Why? Because he knew it would make his dead mother sad, he said, the same sadness that led her to kill herself."

As a Christian, he believed in an afterlife, a place where his mother would be less burdened by sorrow. A devout Christian herself, Elliott knows that for some, the unseen element that gives their life purpose is the god of their faith. For others, she knows religion is a source of mistrust, perhaps abuse, or maybe something that was used vengefully against them. Regrettably, she acknowledges that religion presents children with what she calls "a malignant paradox," something that can be harnessed for great good but also corrupted to justify hatred and exclusivity.

God, and one's life's purpose, cannot, however, be ignored. The spiritual is like an elderly parent whom we phone every day, whom we talk about lovingly, whom we visit every weekend. How could we ignore such a powerful presence in people's lives?

Even very young children have a sense of connection to something beyond themselves. They know that being good matters, and that being bad puts distance between them and the people who love them. As Elliott likes to say, "You don't have to believe in God or trust in God. You just have to find someone a little slicker than you are!"

"I like that," says Katherine. "I don't know, though, if Amanda has any sense of anything except her own selfish wants."

"I'm sure she's a better kid than that," Tina says, offering her support.

"It's not nice to say, but honestly, that's how she acts."

"Making a child feel like she belongs isn't always easy," I say. "We all know that and share your confusion, Katherine. I have some suggestions that may help." I turn to the flip chart and start writing.

Practise Quiet

Stop lecturing your children. Stop telling them all about the world as you understand it and let them tell you about the world as they experience it. The more they talk, the more likely they are to feel a part of your life. They will feel their home is a safe place where they can share their truths.

Listen Attentively

Listen to their music (at least a little). Listen to what they have to tell you while you drive them to the mall or to dance class. Listen to what they say to their friends when their friends are in your car and in your home. Have them teach you how to text or ask permission to visit their Facebook page. Find ways to connect in ways that make sense to them.

Stay Still

Make yourself physically present when you can. Place yourself in the family room where the children play rather than your much quieter office or living room. Join your children in the kitchen for a late-night snack or wait for them after a game and go for a meal, just you and them. Slow down. Make yourself available so they can find you even before they know they need you.

Share Yourself

Invite your children to join you in the activities you find meaningful, whether that be attending a religious service or watching the cooking channel. Both are good. The important thing is to open up doors so that they can enter into your world.

Be Proud

Children like to be part of families that are proud of who they are. Show your child what is fabulous about your family and she is more likely to want to join. What is unique about you as a group? Your backyard trampoline? Your vacation to the Florida Everglades? Your passionate belief in aliens? I'm always surprised at the small and not-so-small things that make children identify proudly with their families.

Explore Your History

For children to feel connected to their families, it's helpful if they know their family story. Where are they from? How did they get here? Why did their ancestors emigrate? What did their ancestors do that was special?

Katherine says, "I talk about our family struggles with Amanda. The bad luck we've had. All those things you just wrote down, they sound so positive. But I let Amanda know she comes from a long line of survivors. I'm always reminding her that she has something special inside her. We know how to fight back when we're knocked down. Sometimes, though, I wish I hadn't told her that. When she's arguing with me, or not listening, I think maybe it's because she knows her family is like that. We're strong-willed when we have to be."

"There is something about passing along family stories, good and bad, that fortifies children. Though Amanda may be a handful now, I bet she'll be stronger later for having heard she comes from a family of fighters,'" I say.

"I think it's the routine things we do," says Merlinda. "You know, the holiday decorating. And Sunday dinners with a centrepiece on the table. I think it's those kinds of things that connect children to their families."

"Great point," I say. "But if I could add one thing to what you just told us, it would be that those routine times also have to be times during which children are heard, stories told, and a sense of belonging nurtured. I've seen families offer lots of routine and the kids rebel, usually associating those times together with being yelled at, lectured, or punished when they didn't do everything they were told in exactly the way their parents expected. No wonder some children grow up rejecting their parents' traditions and culture and even denying their ancestral roots."

"And what if your kid tells you he'd prefer to belong with his friends than at home with his parents? What then?" asks Ricky, his arms tightly crossed.

"That's a good question, too. My own way of handling that with my kids has been to gently insist that my children participate in family events. In other words, I provide some structure and reasonable expectations. Our holiday dinner is not optional. But I'm careful to make the occasion one where they feel connected. Maybe it's asking them to help cook, or making sure I tell everyone who gathers about something special that each of my children has done so they can become the centre of attention for a while. Or maybe it's inviting a grandparent to tell a story, something that will interest my children."

The room begins to buzz with chatter. Seems everyone can remember some special dinner, or special person, who helped connect them to their family while growing up. It wasn't always their parents, either. A stepgrandfather, an older cousin, an uncle, or friend of the family, they can all make children feel special and welcome.

As the group becomes more reflective, I share a story about a remarkable experience I had visiting a group home for adolescent boys who had sexually offended. If ever there was a place for children pushed from their families and communities, this is it. Most of these boys suffer the debilitating effects of fetal alcohol syndrome, have attention deficit hyperactivity disorder, are socially awkward, and sexually impulsive. This is a population that is quickly excluded and told never to return. I don't blame people, though, for rejecting these boys. But excommunicating them doesn't make their problem behaviours go away.

Fortunately, the group home gives the boys exactly what they need. First, it provides a milieu that is very structured and full of expectations. It also, even more importantly, makes a long-term commitment to the six boys who reside there at one time. I was stunned to hear that once placed, the boys don't have to leave until after they turn eighteen, and even then, group-home staff will do what they can to smooth a boy's transition back into his community.

If treatment works, and it does, it is not just because the boys get intensive psychotherapy and are taught how to behave. It's because they find at the group home something called "continuity of attachment." People are there for them, now and into the foreseeable future. The group home is their home. They can even, remarkably, bring home a girlfriend or boyfriend if they like and introduce them to the staff. This is a house where they are treated like normal children, not as offenders.

Maybe that's why the kids, for the most part, don't run away. Their workers make the home safe. It feels like a loving place. People accept them while working very hard to ensure they never again offend. Looking in from the outside, the group home looks like a well-functioning family, with solid family values and connections to home, school, and community. The boys are expected to help around the house. They are asked to look after each other. For once, their lives are anchored to solid ground and have meaning.

"Let me see if I got this, then," Frank says. "If our kids feel like their lives have some higher purpose, like someone — maybe us parents — is relying on them, and they feel like they belong at home, in school, and in their communities, they stay out of trouble? Even kids with really big problems."

"Too simple?" I ask.

"No, it makes sense and all, but I can't believe people don't already know this. Why didn't we know this?" Frank stares at his wife. "Merlinda and I, we're smart people. We could have saved Sadie. We let her down, didn't we?"

"Please, don't be harsh on yourself." The entire group echoes the same sentiment. "Most of us don't know this. Or, we forget what we knew as children made us feel connected and whole. You're not alone in your forgetfulness. I do it. We all do it."

Frank sits quietly saying nothing more. The silence is unusually awkward, like we're waiting for someone to leave a public washroom. There's a strange embarrassment at something out and in the open that should be less public.

"There's another part of belonging that we give our children that we haven't spoken about yet. That's our culture. And it's very important. I know this because my friend's eight-year-old daughter is caught between cultures. Her parents are second-generation immigrants who returned to Pakistan in their late teens, met, married, had their daughter, Amber, and reluctantly agreed to come back to North America because of the violence in Pakistan's northern Swat Valley, where they'd settled. I've been there. It's an idyllic Shangri-La hill station a few hours north of Pakistan's capital, Islamabad. It used to be a romantic setting, with its winding roads and backdrop of snow-capped Himalayas. It's not the same anymore, having become contested territory in the war against the Taliban. But ten years ago, it was a land where you could imagine princesses walking.

"Despite the beautiful stories of her rich heritage, Amber felt awkward when she was told to wear her traditional Pakistani clothes to school. 'You should be proud of who you are,' her mother told her, but Amber avoided the brightly coloured *shalwar kameez* — the long tunic and baggy pants fashioned from festive cloth. When her grandparents came for a visit, however, there was no getting around it. 'Do it for your *nana* and *nani*,' her mother pleaded. The next morning she went to school, her tummy a rumbling mess, dreading what her classmates would say.

"That afternoon, though, she came home — eyes big black saucers — hopping from foot to foot. Proudly, she told her grandfather, 'The other girls thought I looked beautiful.'"

I shake my head. "Strip children of their culture and you leave them naked among their enemies. That's what I've learned." Tina and Ricky nod enthusiastically. This is something I'm sure they understand. It's much less clear to Katherine, Merlinda, and Frank.

"I don't know if I have a culture to pass to Amanda," Katherine says. "Excuse my ignorance, but isn't culture something that people have when they first come to this country?"

"Culture is sometimes hard to see when you're in the majority. But even children from families who are white and speak only English — with grandparents or great-grandparents whose roots are in Great Britain, Scandinavia, Germany, Italy, and France — they, too, need to know about their past. Every family has some traditions handed down from one generation to the next." I pause while everyone thinks about that.

"Do you have any special celebrations? Do you cook any special foods? Even better, do your children know where their grandparents come from?"

"We were Ukrainian. And I think it was my great-grandfather who settled on the prairies. But you really think any of that can make Amanda behave better?"

"Not by itself, no. But like I said — what families have taught me is that when kids look for something powerful to say about themselves, develop a sense of justice, and go in search of some way to take control of their lives, culture becomes a big part of the answer to their problems.

"Think about this: Amanda comes home after school, alone, and she has decisions to make. What is she going to do? Study, play, or hide at a friend's? A child who has heard stories about her grandparents' struggles is going to feel like choosing to study honours their sacrifices. A child who is told about how sturdy and hard-working her grandparents were might decide to not study and instead think about getting married, raising a family, or going to work very young. In other words, children use their cultural heritage to help shape their decisions. Jemell uses his when he decides whether to fight or talk his way through problems. And Sadie, I'm worried, may not know enough about her family history to let it help her make any decisions at all."

"You're right about that," says Merlinda. "She doesn't really know where she comes from. It's like she's making up her own culture. All that ugly dark makeup."

Katherine surprises us all when she begins to cry. As I go to apologize for upsetting her, she wipes my words to the side. "No, it's all right. I ... just ... wondered ... if I made a mistake coming east. Amanda had friends where we lived before. She was doing well in school. She liked the space. You know what I mean? Prairie towns have lots of space. She could roam. She liked to roam. She liked being driven in boxes of old trucks on farms with her friends. But when we came here, she had to do what I told her to do. It was dangerous. She knew no one."

"That's the thing with culture," I explain gently. "It's a big, warm blanket to wrap ourselves in. We know what's expected. It brings us relationships. An identity. A sense of belonging."

"But what you call culture, that can also be a pretty closed club," says Ricky.

"You're right," I say. "With culture also comes xenophobia, the mistrust of others who are different. Even today, there are cross burnings and other displays of racial and ethnic hatred in our communities. And for what? To prove one group is more right than another? The more I've travelled, the more I'm certain that we need to teach our kids to respect others if we are to raise healthy, happy children."

"I always thought of culture as something pretty conservative," says Frank. "You know, resistant to change. No offence, Katherine, but the church where our family goes isn't too keen on women divorcing their husbands. Or vice versa. That's culture, too, isn't it?"

"I don't think I'd like your church," says Katherine.

I jump in before an argument begins. "Culture may pull people back to the old ways, but it has a remarkable ability to change. Merlinda, I'm guessing you didn't dress like Sadie dresses when you were young."

"God, no!"

"Culture helps guide what we do and sets the everyday rules, but those rules are negotiable. For example, there was a study of African-American mothers that found a certain amount of conflict in their relationship with their children was actually helpful. Those strained relationships seem to be necessary for some kids in some families to grow up and become more independent. But it's not necessarily the same for white families, Native families, or families from Latino backgrounds. And even then, not all black mothers are the same. To understand a cultural pattern, we need to take the time to understand the space in which people live and why one pattern makes sense and another doesn't."

"So, Sadie is in a tug of war with Frank and me. Is that what you're saying? Her culture against our culture."

"You're close. In fact, it is never one or the other. Culture is never yours or mine. We are always negotiating. Sadie needs to know her roots and how those roots can help her make sense of her life. But you also, as her parents, need to understand her culture and the changing world she lives in. It's been said that every culture is in certain respects like all other cultures, like some other cultures, like no other culture. We're all similar, and yet very different. Our kids need to live with that confusion and figure out who they are in spite of it."

"Can you give me an example?" asks Tina.

"My favourite is the fact that over 70 percent of the world's children speak more than one language. In other words, language skills are part of most children's culture. It's something that makes them resilient. Now imagine if our textbooks on child development were written by people in India, a country with sixteen official languages. Culturally they would think North Americans are very backward, our culture perhaps underdeveloped, insular because most of us speak only one language. Of course, that's an outsider's view. We don't think of ourselves that way at all."

"So, we're all different," says Tina.

"And all alike," adds Frank. "We all have some form of worship, right?" They take a moment to look at each other, as if there's something in the others they hadn't seen before.

"You've got it. Of course, globalization is blurring cultural boundaries. We all watch the same reruns of *The Simpsons*."

"What has this to do with our families?" asks Katherine.

"A lot. We need to make our families places where children can feel they belong no matter how different they are. Ask yourself, Katherine, when Amanda comes home, does she have any reason to believe her home is where she belongs? That she's needed there? That her life has a bigger purpose, for her and for you? That this is where she has roots?"

"We've moved so much.... It's been difficult. And I'm not there after school." She sounds lost.

"You said earlier, though, that you were fighters. And fighters know how to survive even when they're refugees. I don't have any simple answers, but it strikes me that somehow, Amanda needs to know she's needed at home, that you not having to worry about where she is after school would help you, as a family, survive, and that her home, even if it is only a temporary place to live, is still a place where she can connect with you. It may take some dramatic changes in your family routine — like eating dinner much later or spending every Sunday doing something together — but somehow you and Amanda need to help each other survive." Katherine settles pensively, deep in her seat.

Outside the street lights show the first dusting of new snow. It will be a cold drive home.

"I didn't mean to bring everyone down even more tonight. My point is that children need a sense of belonging, spirituality, and life purpose. Those are hard things to give them."

"You didn't bring us down," says Tina. "What you're talking about is true. It's why we've got our church. It's an anchor through difficult times. Always has been."

"I'm not a churchgoer myself," says Katherine, breaking from her trance. "But I hear what you're saying. My Amanda, she needs a place where she belongs. All our moves, and the loss of her father, I'm not sure I've given her that. But you make me think that I can."

"It's never too late to start, is it?" I say and hand out another cue card. All the while, I'm watching Merlinda and Frank, who sit choking back tears, their hands clasped together, bracing themselves for what's next.

Things Our Children Need
7. A Sense of Belonging, Spirituality, and Life Purpose

- Our children need to know they belong in their families, as well as at their schools and in their communities.
- Our children need parents who will help them shape their values and beliefs.
- Our children need to believe their lives have a purpose and that their families need them.
- Our children need to know their culture in order to better understand who they are.

I think for a moment about suggesting we hug goodbye. Tonight, it feels like we could all use an ending that's a little more intimate. But I wonder if everyone will think I'm being silly or unprofessional. I shrug the thought away and shake hands instead. Still, it's good to feel Tina's left hand placed high on my shoulder as we shake with our right. We lean toward one another, but that's all, then say good night.

Next it's Katherine's turn. Her handshake is firm.

Even Frank extends his leather mitt toward me. "Let's talk later this week," I tell him. "I'd like to know how Sadie is doing." He nods and lets go.

Merlinda takes my right hand in both of hers, looking down at our clasped fingers like a priest in prayer. She says nothing, though her lips tremble with what sounds like a silent blessing. With my hand still warmly in hers, my spine tingles and I know that whether we would have wished to be here or not, this group has become our second home.

Chapter 13

The Eighth Thing Children Need — Rights and Responsibilities

I'm no saint. I've struggled like most everyone else to be as good a father to my children as I can be, and fulfill my responsibilities. The trouble is I've always been afraid of mediocrity. Routine bulldozes my soul, leaving me feeling empty and exposed. I am a happy manic in a world where I was told by my father to settle for the predictability of a twenty-five-year mortgage, whole life insurance, and a pension.

If I'm completely honest with myself, my greatest fear has always been becoming too much like him. Though he had tried to be Bagel Man for a little while — even in our new house, his truck parked outside — I remember him on many a Sunday afternoon looking over bank statements and arguing with my mother. He looked like a farmer whose crop wouldn't grow, his face more wearied and grey over time, not from the relentless sun, but from too few smiles.

Travel has helped make me feel different from him. It shatters routine, though there are times I wake up in a hotel room, and for the first few seconds, I don't know what city I'm in. Beijing? Dar es Salaam? Delhi? Chicago? London? Home draws me at times like those. All the innocent flirting I do in my mind thinking about a different life is just a distraction that reminds me I have the choice of being anywhere I want to be, with whomever I want to be with. My imaginings always end the same: I stay faithful to the snug routine of belonging where I feel most needed. These days I am always happy to come home where my partner let's me know how much she loves me (and I remember at her touch how very much I love her).

It's four weeks before we hold our next meeting. That's lousy timing given what just happened to Sadie. I had warned the group, though, that my work would require me to go to Colombia in late November.

This time, I take my children and we extend my time there to include a week at an ecolodge 120 kilometres down the Amazon from the airport in Leticia. We arrive in the middle of the night, stepping out of the narrow wooden motorboat into mud, then feeling like we've entered the set of *Survivor* as we make our way up hand-hewn steps to the main lodge, which is perched on stilts. Kerosene torches light our way.

The next morning, we wake to find a cockatoo sitting on the railing beside our door. Then over breakfast, we watch freshwater dolphins feed at the shore and look for snakes in the tree canopy that surrounds our hut. Remarkably, a satellite link brings me Wi-Fi two hours a day when the staff run the generator.

I know the women in the Last Problem Child Group have been exchanging emails. Frank and Ricky have spoken by phone at least once. They don't normally include me in these circles of support, so I'm surprised when I get an email from Tina. "Jemell is struggling, but that can wait. You should talk with Merlinda and Frank right away."

I quickly open Skype on my computer and place a call to Merlinda's home number. Through my headset I hear her worried voice say, "Sadie's pregnant." Then she starts crying. The news brings tears to my eyes, and my children, sitting a little ways away, are wondering why I suddenly look so sad.

"The assault?" I mumble quietly, hoping Merlinda can hear me.

"No, it's got nothing to do with her being assaulted. It ... it ... happened before that. Maybe two, three weeks before." Her sobs tear at my heart like razor blades.

"Merlinda, I'm so sorry to hear this. I'm not in Canada, but when I'm back, we can meet."

"It's all right," she says, catching her breath. "I've been talking with Tina and Katherine. Oh, Frank is furious, of course. But he's promised not to say anything to Sadie until he's calmed down. He's letting me discuss the options."

"Options?"

"I don't know. I want there to be options. She's so young to have a child. The embarrassment ... I know I shouldn't say that, but I'm so ashamed. It's like this is all about me. I've failed."

"You haven't failed," I tell her. Then I pause. The line has a strange echo. It feels cold to offer sympathy from this distance. "When I'm back, we can talk. Just remember, she needs you."

"That's the strangest thing. She actually said that. 'I need you, Mom,' that's what she said. It made me cry...." Through the static I hear Merlinda sniffling. "It's the first time in a long time she's actually come to me for help. She sat next to me and cried. It was so strange. Having her back at my side and letting me stroke her hair. Oh my God, I missed doing that. And I was so angry with her. But I just did nothing. No lecture. Like you'd said. I kept all my worries to myself just then. I just sat and combed my fingers through her hair and told her everything was going to be all right...."

"Merlinda?" The line breaks up after that and I give up after two unsuccessful tries to reconnect. I've been listening so intently I haven't even felt the ants crawling up my legs. Now a fiery itch makes me jump up and start scratching.

"Damn," I shout. But then what have I really to complain about? My own daughter is here with me, splashing cold water on my legs, trying to help take away the sting.

Here in the jungle with me, at least I know she's safe.

Ricky storms into my office first thing on the Monday morning that I get back. "Fix him before I kill him," he tells me. Jemell lopes in behind him, then Tina, obviously exasperated with both men in her life. It's going to be a busy week, I can already tell.

"He doesn't go to school. He's fifteen. He has to go to school."

"He's not doing his chores, either," says Tina. "He has a clothes hamper but he still doesn't put anything in it. He needs to take responsibility for these things."

For a moment I'm about to say something to Ricky and Tina about Sadie, but Tina points a finger at her son, as if to say 'Focus on this one for now.' I agree. Sadie's business is better kept for our group time together.

There's a lot to talk about with Jemell. Dirty clothes look easier than chronic truancy. I take one big breath and plunge back into my role as family therapist.

"So I guess Jemell will have to wash his clothes himself."

"I'll do better than that," Jemell yells. "If they want, they can let me move out. I'll go live with my uncle. He'd f——ing stay out of my stuff."

"How about we set some ground rules," I insist. "No swearing. But I promise, Jemell, I'll get your parents to hear what you have to say." I hope I'm modelling a little of how to handle a kid like this. Be firm, but also let him know I'm willing to listen.

"We don't want you to move out. Just take more responsibility for yourself," says Tina.

"That's not all he's got to do," says Ricky. "After what he did to me, I'm thinking a little time away would be a good idea."

"What did he do?" I ask, bracing myself.

"He spit in my face and put his fist through his door." I can sense danger creeping into the room. Jemell looks ready to explode, kneading his right fist in his left palm.

"Yeah, but this crazy motherfu—" Jemell stops before he finishes the word, showing me that he is willing to respect my office rules, at least for now. "My parents don't know what I go through living with them. My dad was on top of me and choking me. Then I was like, 'I'll have to damn well smack you if you don't get off,' and then my mom came in and I threw my dad off and he is, like, blaming me for being violent. That's bull, plain bull."

"I had to grab him. He was gonna bust every wall in the house. I wasn't choking him intentionally. I was trying to stop him," Ricky says, his tone somewhere between frustration and the embarrassment that comes with being outmanoeuvred by your teen.

"It's a dangerous line to cross, isn't it?"

"What else was there to do? Call the cops? Make my son feel even more like a criminal?"

"I won't stay at home if he does that crap. I'm out of there."

"But we want you at home, Jemell," Tina says, worried her family is about to fall apart. "And you have to go to school."

There's no use talking now about the skipping, but since it's been raised, Jemell starts arguing. "I ain't going to go to school if I keep getting called out to fight just because I'm black. I gave up fighting. I done that for you two, but you haven't noticed anything I've done. All you see is my not going to class."

"Jemell, I think they have seen you change. They've been listening when you tell them about how you're treated. Your dad knows what it's like to experience racism."

"They haven't seen shit," Jemell says, sounding very much alone and childlike. I ignore the swearing for the moment.

"Seems, Michael, like the more we try, the less he notices." Ricky is having trouble looking at me and stares at the floor. His voice softens. "I don't know, maybe nothing will work. We keep telling him to tell the principal if he's picked on but he won't. We can't get him to do anything," Ricky says, then pauses. Maybe he's thinking about his own childhood. "I think he's using the racism as an excuse to stay out of class and avoid studying." Jemell rolls his eyes. "Maybe he should go find someplace else to live where people will treat him more fair and not make him go to school."

At the mention of being asked to leave, Jemell explodes. "See what I put up with? They don't even want me at home. No wonder I get into fights, why I can't study. I'm so wound up all the time." He's standing up now. "The hell with it. After this meeting, I'm telling you, I'm gone. I'll take the money you leave in the car and turn that little bit of f——ing change into more money than both you f——ers have." Ricky starts laughing. "Why you laughing?" yells Jemell.

"Because it's stupid," Ricky says.

"It's not stupid. It's you who's f——ing stupid."

At this point I stand up and hold my hands out to stop them both from speaking. "Enough," I tell them. "This is a place where we solve problems, not make them bigger." They both quiet. Thankfully, Jemell sits back down. Tina takes one deep, heavy breath.

"Let's get this clear. Do you want your son at home?" I ask.

"Yes, of course," Ricky says, glancing at Jemell, who is looking at the ceiling, hands clasped behind his head like a boxer between bouts. "But he can't be violent, and he has to go to school."

"Yeah, yeah, yeah."

"Well, let's see if I can find something everybody wants. Besides keeping Jemell at home. Jemell, you want to be treated more like an adult?"

"Yeah. But I can move out if they don't get that."

"So how about we talk about what your parents would see you doing if you were an adult. How will they know that you can take responsibility for making your own decisions?" It's a simple question, but it works. Jemell calms down and tells us that he'll look after his room himself. He'll do his laundry if he forgets to place his dirty clothes in the hamper outside his door. But he'll also make decisions about who comes into his bedroom, including his girlfriend. I like the negotiation.

"This is the same girlfriend whose father hates you?" I ask.

"Uh-huh," he says.

"See, the boy has beans for brains," says Ricky.

"I think this is something that your parents have to have some say over. Not who you date, but whether they feel comfortable having her in your bedroom in their house. There needs to be a balance here, between your right to do what you want, and your responsibility to make your family feel comfortable with things that could affect them. What do you think?" Jemell grunts, but doesn't push the issue further.

Tina jumps in with her mouth wide open. "We know what those two are up to, and while I'd rather they not be, what's done is done. Best now to just make sure there's no pregnancy. I know that sounds awfully slack on our part, but what are we going to do about it?" At the mention of his sex life, Jemell smirks but says nothing. None of us trust that Jemell will practise safe sex, but Tina is right. If we adults don't start talking to Jemell like an adult, and treating him like one, then he's going to get himself, and his girlfriend, into more serious trouble, like a pregnancy.

"Okay," I say, looking for a compromise. "So maybe he can have his girlfriend over, but how about that also means her father knows."

"No problem," says Jemell. "We're not afraid of him. He's chilled a bit since that thing at the store." That thing was a red thong, and my guess is Dad hasn't chilled one bit. But this will be Jemell's problem to solve. Tina and Ricky, however, will be phoning the girl's dad so that he's aware of where his daughter is. If he doesn't want her there, then that's his problem, not theirs.

"I know it seems like kids are always whining about their rights but the truth is that the kids who are most likely to have problems are those who are least likely to be treated fairly."

The parents all guffaw. "You'll have to prove that one to me," says Ricky. The group members are all here tonight and happy to watch me deal with Ricky's challenge.

For Merlinda and Frank, it's a distraction from their own problems. They made it clear at the beginning of the group as we checked in that they would rather talk about something other than Sadie and the pregnancy tonight. They'd done lots of that over the phone and in coffee shops and bars the past week or two with the other parents. "We want to look toward the future," Merlinda said. "What we can do to rescue Sadie from getting into even more trouble."

"I think we need to teach our kids the right way to stand up for themselves," I say, addressing Ricky's taunt. "And that means teaching them to stand up to us and our rules at home first. It's a great place for them to practise. It's safe. They can make mistakes."

"My Jemell," says Tina, "he needs to understand he's a black boy living in a white world. We teach him at home how to talk back when people put him down because of his skin colour. Is that what you mean? That we need to teach our kids about social justice at home, so they can protect themselves when they're at school?"

"I couldn't have said it better."

Katherine says, "My problem is a little different. Amanda talks back to me all the time. Are you saying that's good? That I should teach Amanda to *not do* what I tell her to do?"

"No, not at all. Please don't misunderstand. It's not about teaching a child to refuse our rules or to be rude and belligerent. What I'm saying is that we need to show children how to insist they are treated fairly. That means teaching them to respectfully negotiate rules with us."

I ask the group to consider how they learned to stand up for themselves and who taught them the skills they needed to do that.

"I was never very good at that at all," says Katherine. "I've been in awful relationships with men who just used me."

"So what do you want to teach Amanda?"

"I want her to not take crap from anyone," she says, grinning. The rest of the group joins her with their smiles. "Especially men." I like what Katherine's just said. I'd say the same thing about my own daughter.

"We can teach our children those skills. Here are some examples of ways I've seen families teach children about their rights without turning them into selfish brats." I write points on the flip chart, explaining each one as I go along.

Conflict Between Siblings

Fighting between siblings may drive parents nuts, but it also offers an opportunity to teach children how to stand up for their rights and negotiate their way through conflict without becoming violent. For example, a younger child who never gets his fair share of dessert can be given the choice of either cutting the cake or choosing his slice first. Either way, he'll learn that there are solutions to conflict that don't involve whining or yelling to get his own way.

Sibling Rivalry

There are times when it can appear parents favour one child over another. Many of us grew up understanding that the older child always got the new bike and the younger one got the hand-me-down. There is nothing wrong with teaching children that *equal* doesn't mean everyone necessarily gets the same thing every time. The older child gets a new bike because he grew. The younger child may have other privileges, like more time with Mom and Dad reading bedtime stories. As parents, we can make our homes spaces where children learn that justice means getting our needs met, but it doesn't mean all people's needs are the same.

A Weekly Allowance

Money is a great way to teach children about rights and responsibilities. I hesitate to pay a child to do chores because it tells the child she's not an equal member of her family. A family member has obligations to help other family members. No one pays me to cook dinner. No one should pay a child to clean her room or walk the dog.

An allowance is, however, a very powerful tool to teach children about responsibility, money management, debt, and the value of what they earn. It is also a way to help children understand what it means to have enough or too little. It's particularly important that children use their own money to buy gifts for others during the holidays or on birthdays. That's a great way for them to learn how to make decisions regarding what they can and can't afford. A child who does that is not likely to be a child who teases others about their clothing or what vacations their family can afford.

The Bullied Child

Bullying is more than a single episode of your child being hurt. It is sustained harassment that targets your child specifically. A child who is bullied can learn to talk back to the bully, defend his rights by telling adults what's going on, or — best of all — find a friend who will stand by him. These are good strategies to learn as a child. Learning to stand up for himself or protect himself when the bully is much stronger than he is are skills your child will find useful later at his workplace, with his in-laws, and with his neighbours.

The Shy Child

In our hyperactive culture, we can sometimes trample the rights of a shy child to have few friends and spend time by herself. I always ask parents with shy children to first convince me of the danger a withdrawn child faces. If the child is completely isolated, then it is a parent's job to help the child find friends. But respecting a child's rights means not pushing the child more than she is comfortable being pushed. The hockey parent may not understand the daydreaming youngster who prefers reading to goaltending, but that doesn't mean the child must necessarily change.

The Rude or Surly Child

Children who are disrespectful toward others need to learn that everyone has rights, including the right to be spoken to with respect. Children often behave this way because that is how they are treated by others (for example, their parents swear at them, then tell them not to swear) or because no one has set firm boundaries on their behaviour and guaranteed the consequences. A child who speaks to me rudely, and denies me my right to be treated fairly as an adult, is not going to get any favours from me.

The Out-of-Control Child

A child who is out of control needs structure and consequences, not punishment. A child has the right to personal integrity, which means she has the same rights as anyone else to not be hit, humiliated, or abused. An out-of-control child has the right to expect others will put her in her room, insist she obey some basic rules, and not hurt others. She also has the right to be told what she must do — and shown calmly how to do it — to make amends to those she's hurt and to improve her behaviour so she can participate again in activities with others.

I explain, "None of these strategies are easy, but they all teach your child how to respect others. Children learn from watching us parents model respectful ways of solving problems. That's why I don't like corporal punishment. It teaches children that big people can hit little people. It says some people are entitled to hit others, and others are victims. Where does the logic end? Does a man have a right to hit a woman if they are married just because he's bigger than she is?"

"Sounds like we're back to what we learned before," says Merlinda. "Structure and consequences. Only now we're using both to teach children about their rights."

"Exactly. The nine things children need from their parents are part of the same puzzle. Our children need them all. Imagine giving a child consequences that the child felt were completely unfair. It doesn't work. It breeds resentment. It teaches a child nothing about how to behave. However, if your child can argue for her rights at home, think about how good she'll be at standing up for herself when she encounters really nasty people who want to take advantage of her. Say at work, in a long-term relationship, or with her peers. That will be the kind of kid who can avoid problems and get what she needs without harming herself or anyone else."

Frank says, "I vote. I'm not a racist. Isn't that enough? How can I teach Sadie about standing up for her rights? For God's sake, our home isn't the United Nations."

"What you're showing her by your own behaviour is a very good start, Frank. But if you really want your daughter to avoid big problems, the answer is a little more complicated." I can feel my stomach knot. I'm choosing my words very carefully, not wanting to offend Frank or anyone else. "You have to be sure your child practises what you preach. You vote. Then shouldn't your daughter have a vote over where you go for your summer holiday? You're not a racist. Then shouldn't Sadie's friends be shown tolerance for their differences? I'll bet Sadie will defend every last one of them if she feels cornered and that you don't respect her choices."

There's doubt on everyone's faces except Tina's. "I think you're right about that," says Tina. My stomach unknots. I could give her a hug for saying what she just said.

Ricky looks at his wife, then stretches his legs out in front of him and places both palms on his thighs. "Hang on a minute. Are you saying our kids are always right? Jemell's a punk-ass little kid that needs some control."

"I hear you," I say. "I'm not saying we have to *agree* with our children's choices. They're often not great, are they? But we do have to show our children how to respectfully voice disagreement. So, let me ask you, Ricky, how do you get Jemell to think about what he does without making him feel like he's stupid?"

"Well, that's the thing. We don't know what to say to him that will stop him from becoming more of a badass than he already is. Heck, the police know who my son is. That's not a good thing."

"If you think about Jemell's life as Jemell experiences it, then the question is, if he wasn't a badass, as you put it, what else could he be that would get him some respect? That kind of question takes us right back to the three principles I discussed the first night we met. Remember? *There are children with problems, but they are not problem children; a well-cared-for child will grow up well;* and *children need to be problem free and flourishing.*"

"So what you're saying is that beneath it all, he's a good kid who thinks he doesn't have any other way to succeed except by being a bad kid."

"Yes, that's what I think."

"Maybe he could go to work? But who's gonna hire him?"

"That's the problem, isn't it? We yell at our kids to change, but I'm afraid it's up to us adults to create a just world for them to grow up in. Is it really fair that Jemell has been bullied? Is it fair that a young person can't find a job, or that he feels stupid and threatened at school because he has trouble learning? Heck, is it fair that Sadie is told the only way to make an impression on others is to become a sexualized toy for them to play with?"

Everyone is sitting in stony silence. We don't spend much time as parents thinking about racism, sexism, or the doors that close on our children because of where they live and who they are. We tell kids the world is a meritocracy. Be good, study hard, and everything will work out. And it does, for some. But there are still kids who develop big problems because they grow up in worlds that push them aside or expect them to behave in ways that are not in their own best interests.

"What's that look like, then? How can I help Jemell cope with all the crap in his life?" Ricky asks.

"If he can't work, can he volunteer? Can you give him an allowance so he feels like he is responsible for something in his life? Can you find some way of telling him, 'You're getting older, you're a young man. You're not a child anymore'? That's what social justice means. It means we are treated fairly in our families and communities."

"Pardon me for saying this, but he's still a black kid in a white world. I don't care if there's a black president or not, it's still not a fair world."

"That's where you come in. You've done all right. He needs to hear your story. He needs to learn how you made good decisions."

"I had some bad times when I was his age."

"But you changed?"

"I got scared. There was a brush with the police. But after that, I said, 'I'm not gonna waste my life.' I know it sounds clichéd, but it really was like that."

"And then what did you do? After you decided to get your life together?"

"I found work. I told anyone who put me down where they could stuff it. I made some new friends. Then married." He casts a quick, appreciative glance toward Tina. "I guess I found places where I was treated fairly. No one calls me their n——. Sorry. I don't let people use the N-word around me. No one gets away with that."

"I think as parents we want our kids to stand up for themselves when others harass them. You're a good role model in that regard, Ricky." He smiles, appreciating the respect I've just shown him.

"But don't we want them to listen, when they're at home, to us?" asks Frank.

"Can't have it both ways," I say. "Can't tell the kids to do one thing out beyond our front doors and do something different at home. Remember, we're a safe place where they can experiment and learn how to assert their rights and be held accountable for the responsibilities they have to others. We're the best training ground they have."

This entire evening feels like I'm climbing a mountain. Take a few steps, rest, acclimatize to the thinning air, move forward slowly, then stop again. The higher you go, the more clearly you see where you are.

"It's easier for me to show you what I mean with an example." There is a collective group nod. "This is another of those areas lots of parents find uncomfortable. What do we say when our children tell us they're gay, lesbian, bisexual, or transgendered? Though kids these days are much more tolerant of a rainbow of sexual orientations, that doesn't mean that a lot of kids still don't experience prejudice and hatred when they come out." A lot of parents don't support their kids when they are open about their sexuality. No wonder so many young people who run away to the street are those who feel excluded at home, at their church, in their schools, and among their peers.

Robert-Jay Green, executive director of the Rockway Institute, and someone whose work I respect a great deal, has worked with many young people who know first-hand the fear that comes with being called "faggot" and "queer." He's met lots of children who have been told by their folks, "Who you are is wrong." It's not surprising that they turn into runaways or drug addicts, or to suicide as ways to cope with their trampled self-esteem and denial of their basic human rights.

"The solution is the same for these kids as it is for any child who is excluded because he appears different from what we blindly assume a child is supposed to look like and be." I flip to a clean sheet of paper at the front of the room and begin to write as I talk. "In those situations, we need to encourage kids who are told they are different and getting hurt because of it that they have options. They can do lots of things to fight back without raising their fists." I write each strategy, then explain what each means.

Resist!

We need to teach children how to talk back to those who tell them they're not good enough just because they're different.

Tell It Like it Is!

Kids who are told they're different need a safe place to shout "This is who I am!" and be proud of it. I like it when I see kids forming rainbow alliances at their schools, in which straight and gay kids advocate for change and protect one another.

Make Others Change!

There are many families, from Dick Cheney's to that of my colleague down the hall, who have had to get educated about issues of diversity, including diversity in sexual orientation, race, and ability. Schools can change the way they treat minorities, and communities can embrace those with disabilities, just as families can welcome home a child they've excluded because of her sexual orientation.

Ask For What They Need!

Kids who are excluded need to be shown how they can ask for what they need. They need to be believed when they tell their parents and educators about the bullying they experience. They need to know that people like them are part of their communities and that they belong there.

Be Safe!

Children who feel excluded need to know it's safe to be themselves. That means we adults have a role to play in creating safe spaces.

Find a Place to Celebrate Who They Really Are!

If children can't be themselves in one space, then help them find another. If one group of peers rejects them, they need to find others who won't. Of course, our children can't change their parents, which means we'd better look at ourselves as parents. If we're the ones doing the excluding, are we helping our child avoid problems or pushing her toward disaster?

Make Peace!

When all else fails, we can coach our kids on how to make peace with those who won't change. And there are lots of ways. The *Art of War*, China's ancient text on the art of waging war, advises, "Do not attack a fortified castle wall." Sometimes it is better to be strategic and confront what you can change and ignore what only time will starve into reasonableness.

"I like those," says Tina.

Ricky nods. "I want Jemell to know how to do those things rather than always getting into fights."

Merlinda says, "I want Sadie to tell us what she needs. I don't want her to have to run away."

"I think you're getting it. Making sure our children get treated fairly, and teaching them how to negotiate for their rights in reasonable, respectful ways, is a great strategy for helping them stop being kids with problems." The group nods. "It's the same with responsibilities. You don't let people have responsibilities if they have no right to make decisions for themselves."

"Like we've been trying to do with Jemell," says Ricky.

"Exactly," I say, happy to see the connection is being made. "The more Jemell asserts his right to be treated like an adult, the more he will have to take on responsibilities for himself and others. Like doing his own laundry, maybe getting a job, keeping up with his school work, those kinds of things."

"With rights comes responsibilities," Frank adds, echoing a well-worn truth.

"Yup. The more responsibilities Jemell has, and the more we show him we think of him as an adult, the more likely he is to act like someone who is older and our equal."

"And even Amanda wants to learn these things?" Katherine asks. "She's just nine years old."

"I think she does. Only, she is probably thinking more about her rights than her responsibilities."

"Ain't that the truth."

"I haven't talked as much tonight about responsibilities as I have rights because responsibilities are a part of so many of the strategies we've been discussing each week. If you have responsibilities around your home, you feel like you belong. If you have responsibilities to look after someone else, you look in the mirror and see someone important. You feel in control."

Merlinda jumps in. "A word of advice, Katherine. You'd better teach Amanda how to stand up and argue with you while she's still little. Otherwise you could have a child you're worried is lying to you all the time." She pauses and squints, as if trying to see more clearly. "I wish I could roll the clock back a few years. I'd let Sadie argue more. I might even lose an argument now and again so that she'd feel she could talk to me. It's so difficult not really knowing what she's up to."

"I thought things were getting better," I say, aware the group is watching.

"Yes, we say that, but to be totally honest, in my gut I still feel she's hiding something. The way she keeps me out of her room, won't talk to me about anything to do with becoming a young woman, if you understand what I mean. There hasn't been any trouble lately, but why do I feel as if we're at the brink of disaster?"

"Kids," says Ricky. "They drive you crazy no matter what they do."

"I know it can feel like that," I say. "But respect kids' rights, give them lots of responsibilities, and going back to what we learned weeks ago, hold your children accountable for what they're expected to do. They'll feel older, they'll feel you respect them, and they'll feel like they belong in their families. It really works. Trust me on that."

One by one, they slide into their own conversations. Amid the banter, the group begins to break up and I distribute the next cue card.

As Merlinda and Frank get up to leave, I ask them if they'd like to meet soon. "Frank is travelling a lot," Merlinda says.

Frank nods. "When I get back next week, we'll call, or schedule something next Wednesday during the group. There's nothing much to say right now." Merlinda doesn't look so certain, but before we can say any more, Ricky comes over and grabs my hand.

Things Our Children Need

8. Rights and Responsibilities

- Our children need to experience their homes and schools as places where they are treated fairly.
- Our children need to be protected from racism, sexism, and other forms of intolerance.
- Our children need to be shown how they can talk back to people who exclude them or take away their rights. They need to be able to do this without becoming violent.
- Our children need to be given responsibilities at home where they are safe to make mistakes.
- Our children need to be valued for the skills and abilities they have and offered opportunities to use these for their benefit and the benefit of others.

"That was good. Nice to hear someone talk about things like racism. When we've had other counsellors come to talk to us about Jemell, they avoid that kind of thing. I had a school principal once completely deny that my kid was getting called the N-word. Told me *she'd* never heard anyone use the word. She was white, of course. How stupid was that?"

I try focusing on Ricky, but even as I'm telling him thanks for his feedback, my attention is still on Merlinda, who is looking at me as Frank walks her to the door. I wave goodbye and she waves back. "We'll call for an appointment."

I nod and look toward Ricky, but he's turned away and is happily joking with Katherine. I'm suddenly standing there all alone, wondering how much I'm needed after all.

Chapter 14

The Ninth Thing Children Need — Safety and Support

My father loved to drive. And to eat. Not fancy food in restaurants, but homemade food that my mother made. His role was to play the hunter, driving us, in our wood-panelled station wagon, downtown early on wintry Sunday mornings to buy dozens of fresh bagels from the shops on Montreal's Plateau. My mother preferred the bakery on St. Viateur, my father the one on Fairmount with its original storefront and cracked floor tile leading to the open wood ovens. It's still the city's hearth, a half century after my father moved from his boyhood home, which had been only a few blocks west. From the warmth of the shop's doughy air that steamed the windows opaque, we'd come back out into the cold, clean morning air, an entire mixed dozen for us to share in the back seat.

In the fall we'd drive to Rougemont instead, an hour past the last Montreal suburb, looking for twenty-pound bags of apples, homemade pies, and preserves.

Sometimes on hot Friday nights during the summer, my father would go hunting for french fries at a drive-in diner called Normands.

If it was his birthday, or my mother had no time to cook, then it might be a quick jaunt to the Kentucky Fried Chicken store for a bucket. My father always drove and always paid cash, the bills taken firmly one by one from the leather wallet he kept in his front pocket.

Years later, driving my own children home from buying takeout fish and chips (a greasy bag of fries already open and being devoured as we drive), I feel the same as I did growing up, my stomach full and me safely a part of whatever place I call home.

I bring a bag of fresh bagels to the next group meeting. They're chewy and slightly sweet, flown in every day from Montreal. I also buy a tub of cream cheese and a tray of smoked salmon. The group is impressed. "Call it a family tradition," I tell them, then cut the bagels in half and serve them around.

Everyone is here tonight except Katherine. Her babysitter came down with the flu. Katherine is wondering if Amanda is next. "If I have to stay home and look after her ..." Katherine told me on the phone, but didn't finish her sentence. I doubt she can afford to take time off work. I wished her well and hung up. There wasn't anything else I could do.

"Tonight," I tell the group, "I want to talk about the last of the nine important things children need. These are the basics. Things like a warm bed, a hot meal, a safe school, clothes that don't embarrass them, places to play, and opportunities to work if they need money.

"They're not optional. Even the delinquents I work with can be enticed to their parents' dinner tables by the promise of a good meal and the security of knowing they're safe and loved when at home in bed. A child who gets her basic needs met is one who is going to feel good about herself even if she never says thank you to the adults who make her feel that way."

"We can build it, but that don't mean they'll come and get it," Tina says, laughing.

I know exactly what she means. It's not enough to just offer kids the basics. What we offer has to be meaningful to them. Like school. Lots of us adults lost interest in math when we began learning integers. Minus one? "When am I ever going to need this?" we asked ourselves. Soon enough, irrelevance bred contempt, then inattention, and finally failure. Then we felt like idiots and started feeling sick when we had to go to math class.

A lot of delinquent youth have learning challenges. And yet, we are quick to build prisons instead of decreasing student-teacher ratios in our schools. This isn't just bleeding-heart liberalism. Research tells us that schools are a better investment of our tax dollars than prisons. A teacher's aide works for a fraction of what it costs to house a delinquent in a correctional institution.

Instead of well-funded schools, we're witnessing a rapid growth in the correctional-industrial complex, a vast network of penal colonies that imprisons as much as 1 percent of the American population. It's a lousy investment in our future. Funny, but countries that incarcerate people less and provide better education and social support have fewer criminals.

"If I'm anything," I explain to the group, "it's practical. Forget ideology. I want my kids to be safe. Prisons create really scary people who eventually have to live somewhere. Schools produce really interesting people who I'm more likely to want as my neighbours."

I like the way Natalie Proveaux explains it. She's one of the few women who survived the murderous assault by Marc Lépine on December 6, 1989, at Montreal's École Polytechnique. As Lépine stormed into a classroom at the engineering school, he said that he hated feminists and blamed them for taking his seat at the college. Natalie tried to calm him down before he shot her. He killed fourteen women that day before killing himself. Twenty years later, Proveaux is hopeful we've learned something through the tragedy. "The world is full of love," she says, "but horrible things happen to people to make them who they are."

What happened to Lépine to create such a psychopath? It's difficult to know, but we do know that people need safe communities — and schools — to thrive. We know that people who get what they need don't tend to choose antisocial behaviour as a way to solve problems.

It's estimated that you have a one in two million chance of being an innocent victim of gang violence — far, far lower than the chances of being killed driving your child to school every day for a year. By the logic of numbers, we know we are worrying about things we shouldn't. What we should be doing, if we really want to address the problem of gangs, is make sure every child gets to school in the first place. As early as 1927, Frederic Thrasher, in his book *The Gang*, showed us that young men who can't find respect, money, excitement, and power become criminals as a solution to their disenfranchisement. Today, young women do the same.

It's worse for kids who have explosive personalities, impulsivity, need lots of stimulation, or are adventure-seeking maniacs. School is a hard sell when the street holds out hope for so much more.

Sadie, Jemell, maybe even Amanda — they're all looking for something they're not finding closer to home.

The problem with raising kids is we often get our priorities mixed up. We're slogging away to increase our take-home pay, when our kids just want us to show up now and again to watch them bat a homerun in regular-season play.

Charles Dickens had it right when he wrote *A Christmas Carol.* Scrooge is a bitter, rejected man, who replaces his love for others with his love for money. Think of Wall Street bankers purposely duping vulnerable homeowners so they could reap huge, undeserved bonuses. Poverty, as Dickens reminds us, isn't just about poor people failing. It's also about what others do to them that makes their failure more likely.

"A healthy, well-fed child is more awake at school and ready to learn. But children raised in wealthier homes can be at risk, too, when their emotional and developmental needs are ignored."

"So it's not just food kids need. You're saying they need challenges? Risks? That we can disadvantage a child if we overprotect her?" Frank asks.

I nod. "It's easier to see when we're talking about physical neglect. But it's the same for emotional neglect. Children who don't get enough of what they need tend to turn out poorly. That's a simple enough truth. But let me explain. There's some good news and bad news in today's statistics. Overall, we are seeing a decrease in crime among youth. Truthfully, the trend is toward fewer delinquents even though our newspapers make a big deal about the few kids who commit the most crime." The group looks doubtful so I tell them what criminologists all say — a child growing up today is less likely to break the law, less likely to drop out of school, less likely to get pregnant, and less likely to be the victim of crime. One particularly controversial reason for the drop in youth delinquency is that there are simply fewer unwanted children being raised by families that can't afford to keep them. Teenagers have better access to birth control, which means fewer babies are being born. The politics of abortion aside, the fact is fewer children are being raised in families where neglect is almost inevitable.

"Whoa, now," interrupts Tina. "You're saying crime is down because we have more abortions?"

"It's not a popular theory, is it? And I'm not in any way saying that abortion should be the solution, but the fact is, preventing young people who are not ready to parent from having babies means fewer children being brought up in homes that lack the financial and emotional means to raise them. And that means fewer delinquent kids. No ifs, ands, or buts."

"It's a lousy way to control crime."

"On that point, Tina, I would entirely agree. But the point I'm really trying to make is this: if we support our children well, we get healthier teens and adults. How we support them will, of course, reflect our faith and values. However, if our beliefs prevent children from having easy access to contraception or abortion, then doesn't that obligate us to provide the babies who are born with what they need? In other words, we know what to do to stop raising little criminals. Ignoring teen parents is only guaranteeing disaster.

"Maybe we should listen to Dickens. Every child needs a warm bed, a good school, and enough breakfast to get him through the day."

Tina nods uneasily and I change the topic. It's time for a story. This time about a boy named Grant who knows nothing about good breakfasts or a parent with the means to keep him safe. His mother, Caroline, has drunk heavily since Grant's father died when he was just over a year old. His father was an army private stationed overseas when his Jeep was in a traffic accident. Never very outgoing, Caroline withdrew after that. She and Grant have survived on welfare and a small pension. They live in subsidized housing in a rougher part of a mid-sized city on the east coast. Grant was slow learning to read. He entered elementary school barely knowing his colours. The school had him assessed, and by grade two, Grant's mother was told her son had dyslexia. She was encouraged to read to him more and help him with his homework.

Caroline listened and promised to try harder. But instead she occupied her days watching television and drinking away her guilt. Meanwhile, Grant continued to slide. Never a very energetic child, he quickly realized he was different. He was frequently bullied by other boys, who quickly grew bigger than him.

The school noticed Grant slipping quietly through the cracks but the neglect he experienced was never bad enough to get child welfare to take a serious look at the family. Grant had just enough food. He was housed. His mother was there at home to watch him. He went to school most days. Of course, he wore the same clothes day after day, but then so did most other grade threes. The difference was that Grant didn't have a choice. There was nothing else in his closet that fit him.

By grade four, Grant was spending less and less time in a regular classroom. He was placed on a special educational plan and provided a tutor for an hour a day. The tutor tried to include Caroline in the education planning. She'd show up occasionally, but mostly she wanted to talk about herself rather than her son. Grant, Caroline insisted, wasn't doing so badly. He was a good boy. He behaved himself, didn't he? Did as he was told. Ate what she gave him to eat. Never complained.

By age thirteen, Grant had been "socially promoted" to junior high but was reading at a grade-three level, if he read at all. By this time, Caroline was working at a seniors' centre, cooking, as part of a scheme to get her more financially independent. She still drank but managed to do the work required of her. She seemed to be enjoying the time away from Grant. If school conferences required her attendance, she asked that they be scheduled at a time when they wouldn't interfere with her work at the seniors' centre.

Those conferences became more frequent as Grant attended school less often. With his mother out of the house most mornings, Grant preferred to stay home. It was safer there. At school he hated feeling stupid. He hated being teased because of his crooked teeth and cheap clothes. He worried about the boy who had threatened to slit his throat.

These days, Grant spends most of his time in his room. When the school social worker goes to his home to wake him up and drive him to school, Grant doesn't answer the door. His days are spent online, gaming. Caroline insists Grant is old enough to make his own decisions.

"What am I supposed to do?" she asked the social worker. "Drag him out of bed in the morning?"

There are professionals who want to help Grant. There are counsellors and tutors, teachers and social workers. There was even an orthodontist who volunteered his services to help straighten Grant's teeth if he agreed to brush. None of it helped very much. By the time Grant was fifteen, he was attending school only a few days a month. His teeth were brown and full of cavities, the result of a diet that was mostly large bottles of soda and bags of potato chips.

"So, why is this family my problem?" says Frank. Merlinda kicks him, cautioning him to play nice. He ignores her. "I get that we have to provide for people, but in this case, you can't blame everyone else for the boy's problems. His mother is a drunk. She has subsidized housing. What more should we be expected to do for them?"

He's right. We can't endlessly provide resources that don't get used, or are abused or not appreciated. So how do we make sure that children like Grant get what they need and not become the next crop of problem children?

In Australia, they've begun to punish parents who receive state support if their children don't go to school. If they want their welfare checks, their children have to attend school regularly. It works, occasionally, but it also undermines both the dignity and authority of the parents.

"Perhaps we need to think about this more holistically," I suggest. "Rather than punishing people for not doing what they should be doing, we could help them be their best by giving them what they really need. Even Grant told me he would go to school if he felt he could succeed and was sure he wouldn't be bullied." A lot of what children actually need and want cannot be provided by professionals. Grant may have had social workers and special educators chasing him, but we know children need more than professional interventions.

"Let me make this point another way. Gina Browne at McMaster University showed that if you provide the poorest children in a community with access to good recreational activities, like a hockey team, dancing lessons, and a Boys and Girls Club, and even if those activities cost as much as $3,000 a year for each child, there are still short- and long-term cost savings. A healthy, more engaged child needs fewer visits to his family doctor and is much less likely to wind up on the waitlist at the local mental health clinic. Even better, the child who is part of his community is less likely to have the free time, or the inclination, to get into trouble with the law."

"I get what you're saying," Frank tells me, leaning back comfortably in his chair.

"I like that," says Tina. "We all have a role to play in raising healthy kids — and not just our own kids."

"But does what you just said, about Grant, mean that only poor families raise problem kids?" asks Merlinda, straightening the crease of her twill slacks. "I don't think that's true."

"It's a very good point you make. Just providing our children with things won't necessarily prevent them from growing up with problems.

"For example, Suniya Luthar, another researcher, has studied families with annual incomes over $300,000. What she found was that their children still faced challenges, though a lot of the risks they faced had to do with emotionally absent parents, excessively high expectations to perform at school, or demands on them to fit in with the popular kids. In other words, as Merlinda just hinted, a warm bed and a safe street are only useful to a child if the child also feels connected to others and has a powerful identity like we spoke about two weeks ago."

"So, rich or poor, children need the same things. That makes sense," Merlinda says.

"I think so, too, but the trick is finding ways to help that don't embarrass the child or completely bankrupt the state. Let me give you a good example of a program that does work. In one of Toronto's poorest neighbourhoods, Regent Park, an organization called Pathways to Education has been offering every grade nine student help to break the cycle of poverty by getting them to graduate high school. Neither the children nor the parents are punished for not doing what everyone wants them to do. At the start of grade nine, every child in Regent Park, with their parents' consent, is offered a personal mentor who volunteers to meet with the child once a week, access to free after-school tutoring, an advocate to help parents and teachers communicate better, and best of all, a thousand dollars for every year the child stays in the program. That means when children graduate high school four years later, they have a nice nest egg to start college or attend some other type of post-secondary training.

"You might be surprised to know that more than 90 percent of eligible youth take advantage of the program." Eyebrows are raised. "When the program began, only 42 percent of children in Regent Park completed high school. Any guess at the rate of school completion after children participate in the program? And remember, this is an urban slum with the worst rates of drug abuse, teenage pregnancy, and truancy in the city."

"Fifty percent," says Tina.

"Maybe a bit higher," guesses Ricky.

"I was shocked to learn that of the children who participate in the program, 75 percent complete high school. And the story gets even better. Whereas before, only 20 percent of graduates went on to post-secondary education, now 82 percent enrol in college or university. Even more astounding, the Regent Park kids who go to college are likely to have much better attendance records and are much more likely to complete their post-secondary studies than kids from middle-class homes. In other words, the effects of the program linger for years."

"It can't be that simple," says Frank, no longer sitting back in his chair.

"I think it is. I could tell you about lots of other similar programs and quote lots of research like what I've shared this evening. It all says exactly the same thing. We know that when we focus on what epidemiologists call 'the social determinants of health' — like education, health care, recreation, support for families, and safe streets — kids have far fewer serious problems. Instead, though, we keep building prisons. That really worries me because when a child's development gets blocked, that doesn't mean it stops. It simply reroutes. A neglected child, rich or poor, has only so many choices. Like Grant, he can give up. Or he can become a delinquent. Both strategies compensate for something that's very wrong in the child's life. And both choices are entirely preventable."

I stop talking and take time to answer questions. Over and over again, I tell the group, "You need to figure out if your children are getting everything they need."

I ask them to consider questions like

- Are your child's home and school safe?
- Does your child have a private space to study or be alone?
- Does your child have breakfast every day and someone to talk with while eating?
- Does your child have the supports she needs at school?

- Does your child have someone to advocate for her if there is a problem?
- Do you as a family have enough money to get by?

Everyone chuckles as I read the last question.

"Does anyone ever have enough?" Tina jokes.

On my hip, I can feel my cellphone vibrating. I know it will be my daughter needing a lift home from her basketball practice. Her team hasn't been doing very well, which has meant extra practice time. The phone call means our time is up.

"Anything else anyone wants to say?" There's silence. "In that case, let me give you tonight's cue card and I'll see you for the final group meeting next week. That should give everyone enough time to digest those bagels."

Things Our Children Need
9. Safety and Support

- Our children need access to the social determinants of health — things like housing, safe streets, well-resourced schools, and parents with the time to pay attention to them.
- Children, whether rich or poor, who experience physical and emotional neglect tend to grow up with problems. Give children what they need and they are more likely to be problem free and flourishing.
- Children who get their basic needs met, including opportunities to participate in recreational programs, are children who will feel better about themselves.
- Children who feel better about themselves are less likely to need expensive services like mental health clinics, social workers, and prisons.

As everyone leaves, I text my daughter back: "I'll be there in ten minutes." Then I sweep bagel crumbs from the counter and wash the few dishes that are in the sink. As I put my coat on, it strikes me how torn I am emotionally. On one hand, I feel very happy at that moment knowing the group has given us some answers. Even if their children are still struggling, at least the parents are feeling more confident about handling the next crisis, whatever that crisis is.

But there is still much I haven't managed to do. Amanda, Jemell, and certainly Sadie, are not problem free or flourishing. At least not yet. Was it too much to expect that years of conflict could be fixed in just three months? I was naive to hope that everything could be put right so quickly.

I let out a deep sigh and adjust my glasses. "One step at a time," I remind myself as I leave the office, carefully locking the door behind me.

Chapter 15

Endings and New Beginnings

"I know there's a lot to say tonight," I tell everyone as we take our seats. It's our last meeting and I can see on everyone's face a mix of anxiety and anticipation for what's next. Or maybe that's simply how I feel.

Preparing for this evening, I thought about Sadie more than anyone else. I even checked back to see what Sadie had recently posted on Bitches and Babies. I was surprised to find nothing written by G(irl)-Spot, though at least three of the girls were reporting pregnancies. Maybe, just maybe, Sadie is realizing the trouble she's gotten herself into. I'm hopeful that her silence is a sign of better decisions to come even if she is pregnant and, worse still, dealing with the trauma of a sexual assault.

Despite reason for hope, I've been thinking all week how to bring closure to the group and have decided I owe everyone an apology. They trusted me to help them. I know the group has helped a little, but it's not been enough.

"Before we wrap up, I have something important to say," I tell the group. I sit with my shoulders rolled up high but my eyes looking down. It's hard to meet everyone's gaze.

"I think I've failed. I promised you perfect children, free of problems. You trusted me. But I didn't give you what you came here to find." I lift up my head and look each of them in the eye. "I'm so sorry. These are just ideas, from families like yours. But life and our kids are so much more complicated than stories. I'm really sorry if I raised your hopes too high."

I glance at Frank, who is looking oddly at the other group members "He doesn't know, I guess?"

"Doesn't seem so," says Ricky.

"Sadie miscarried," Merlinda tells me. Everyone nods, reassuring me it's true. I sink into my chair, a weight off my shoulders. Was that guilt? Or fear of my own stupidity? Embarrassment at being shown to be so naive with my theories?

"But here's the thing," Frank says. His voice is full of authority. "This is what's strange. We were ready for her to have the baby. I won't lie. I was angry at first — at her, at you. Everyone. I kept thinking, I should have locked her up. Done things my way. Maybe smacked her more when she talked back. All kinds of crazy parenting strategies you've shown us don't work. I know they wouldn't have helped, but I kept blaming myself just the same. And then I called Ricky."

Ricky picks up the story. "I told him to give his head a shake. A good shake. He and Merlinda were on the girl all the time. And all that was happening was she was drifting away from them. Remember?"

"I think it was all the things we've been doing the last couple of months that made Sadie respect us again," says Merlinda. "She came to us for help when she needed it. She trusted us again." Merlinda pats Frank's knee. He cups her hand in his.

"I never thought that girl would go crying to her parents," says Tina.

"I figured you'd go so crazy that you'd kick her out," says Katherine.

"But you didn't," I said.

"No. Something changed," says Merlinda. "Sadie made a big mistake, but she knows it. And here's the really strange thing. We both just knew that even if she'd had the baby, we could have given that child everything it needed. Sadie would have had lots to do, but we were ready, really ready, to accept this as a gift." Merlinda is sobbing now. "We'd have made sure that child had everything it needed. Everything."

"Like some rules," Tina says.

"And lots of love from all three of you," Katherine adds.

"All those things," says Frank. "We just felt we could handle this. That this next child wouldn't have to look for trouble like our Sadie. I know you understand me."

I beam with gratitude. "Yes, I do." Then I ask, "So, how about everyone else?"

"Our Jemell is doing okay. He's coming in on time," Tina tells us.

"Mostly." Ricky corrects her with a nudge.

"Yes, but when he's late or giving us all that gangster crap, we tell him he's got more things to be proud of. He doesn't need to be like that. And it's been working. I think my son is holding his head a little higher these days."

"Helps that he's found some work, too," Ricky says.

"A friend of the family knew the manager at one of those clothing stores at the mall. Now he gets to wear all those crazy fashions and walk around the store looking cool. And he calls that work!" Tina might sound mad, but she isn't really. It's Ricky's turn to nudge her and her frown rises on one side, then the other, and soon we're all laughing along with her.

"A job's a job's a job," Katherine says. "You two should be proud."

"And you, Katherine? How's Amanda doing?"

"She's coming home after school. Once I explained to her I couldn't go to work if I was worried about her and began asking her to help me out, she sort of changed. It was like she appreciated being treated like she was older and had something important to do at home. And the school finally did a psychological assessment."

"Did that help?"

"She has ADHD. Now we'll have to think about the medications. But the school is being more sympathetic since the psychologist identified the problem. I don't know if that's all of it. I still think there are other problems, but for now, they're willing to help and that's just fine by me. They even called me on Monday to say Amanda had a good day. I couldn't believe it. Right out of the blue, they told me something good. Makes me begin to see my daughter in a whole new way."

I can't resist the temptation to reinforce one of the key messages from the group. "That sounds like a powerful identity for a little girl." Amanda is finally being caught doing good things and being treated like she is a fully capable, flourishing child. No surprise that she likes being seen that way and is trying to meet others' expectations.

"I've even asked her if she wants to take the pills and explained what

ADHD is like. You know — fidgeting, easily distracted. I had her stand in front of the mirror when I told her so she could see how she moves all the time. She caught on right away. Now, between you and me, there are going to be consequences if she doesn't take the medications, but no harm in asking her to make the decision herself. Right?"

"No harm that I can see." Of course, the problem will be if Amanda refuses to take her medications. The natural consequence will be that she does poorly at school and continues to be unmanageable at home. Then it will be up to Katherine to make Amanda understand that her behaviour is making it difficult for Katherine to go to work, is causing them to argue, and is making it impossible for her to prepare special meals or for them to have fun times together. Maybe, just maybe, that will be enough to pressure Amanda to stick with her course of medication. Her young age makes me optimistic. It's usually teens who steadfastly refuse to change.

After catching up some more, we take a brief break for coffee. Frank and Ricky stand and stretch, then turn their backs to me and talk in the corner. When we come back together, Frank leans forward on his chair and starts speaking before I can say a word.

"Something still bothers me, Michael. Bothers the rest of us, too."

"What's that?"

"Why my daughter? Other kids get crazy parents like us, and they don't join a bunch of crazy girls and create a pact to get pregnant. They don't run away from home or lie. Why Sadie?"

I give him a sideways frown, grinding my teeth. "It's a hard one to answer. Can you handle a little research?" He nods, but only after checking with Merlinda, then looking around the room at the other group members. They all seem keen to learn.

"Okay," I explain. "Here's what we know." It isn't really that much, but perhaps enough — just enough — to point us in the right direction toward an answer. First, I make it very clear that it's not always possible to save children from bigger problems when our influence on them is just one of many different parts of their lives, and all the others are conspiring to push — or pull — them into trouble. But as I've been saying all along, change a child's environment, and chances are, the child is going to do reasonably well.

"So what makes the difference?" asks Ricky. "Why doesn't every child choose to do well?"

"It's not entirely choice. It's more ... well ... fit, I think. A child looks around and says, 'Hmm, what can I do to survive, and what behaviour is most readily available?'" I explain that a single risk factor, like Sadie going online and participating in a pregnancy pact, can cause a child to have serious problems for years if that one behaviour satisfies the child's need for a powerful identity, self-esteem, relationships, a sense of belonging, and all the other aspects of a child's life we've discussed during the group. But that's only likely to happen if a child like Sadie feels her whole environment is conspiring to close doors to other, more acceptable means of being able to proudly say who she is.

"The real problem is that Sadie swims in a culture that tells young women to become sexual beings very quickly. Though she was hearing lots of different messages at home, I think Sadie may have felt lost, looking for some way to be different from you, her parents. The lowest apple on the branch, the one easiest to reach, was an identity as the girl gone wild."

"We didn't know she was that desperate to be older," cries Merlinda.

"Or at least we've been shy, me especially, to see her like that," says Frank. "Mind you, that's changing. A couple of days ago, I was wrestling to get myself on Twitter, and I asked her to help. But I said, 'I want to show everyone my tweeter.' Well, obviously that wasn't the right way to say what I meant to say and, quick as a wit, Sadie answers, 'I think that's share my *tweets*, Dad. But if you want to show everyone your tweeter ...'" We all laugh at the teasing, pleased to hear Sadie is finding a place for herself at home.

I say, "Maybe it's not just older that she wants to be. Maybe it's stronger, too. More fully adult with the respect that that brings. That would be pretty different from how you used to see her, Frank. Though I'll admit, when it's our own kid, it's hard to see these things clearly. No wonder our own parents often have a lot to say about how to raise their grandkids!" Everyone chuckles, knowing well the helpful and unhelpful intrusions of a doting grandparent.

Tina, however, is not at all satisfied yet. "So if Jemell becomes a gangster, he's imitating what he's told is an easy way to get respect? Like what he sees in music videos?"

"In a sense, yes. But it's not just the videos. You can't blame a single source for such a powerful influence. Think about Sadie. She gets this sexualized message every time she wanders around the mall and looks in store windows or watches any Disney movie. All those princesses sure look young and beautiful and are eventually married off with children of their own. You see, if we want to change our children, we need to think about the environment around them and the protective processes that influence kids. Not just what we provide them at home."

"So," says Katherine, "these, what did you call them? Protective processes? They aren't just something we give our children as parents. We have to change everything around our child, too?"

"Not necessarily, though I wish I had a magic wand and could do just that. But you do have to stack the deck in your favour. Remember, as parents, you still exert a very large influence over your child." What that means, I explain, is that children need lots of exposure to people and experiences that show them what they should be doing instead of exposure to things that are going to show them how to misbehave.

"Of course, sometimes we get stuck. The world beyond our front door is so powerful it overwhelms the messages we give our children. A child can learn lots about healthy ways to problem solve at home, have parents who model compassion, and still have problems."

"You mean," says Ricky, "even if we send our kids to the best schools, live in a great neighbourhood, they can still mess up?"

"It's all about relative influence. When it comes right down to it, you are still a very big part of your child's life, but you aren't the only part. That's why maintaining a relationship with your child is so important. And why providing structure and reasonable consequences convinces your child you give a darn about him. Those are the best ways I know to stack the deck in your favour."

As everyone considers my words, I remind them that we can help provide children with all nine of the things we've discussed their kids need to grow up well. These past many weeks, we've been doing it. Clumsily at first, but improving all the time.

I explain, "The remarkable thing is that even when children are neglected, they can still find these nine things on their own if opportunity knocks. A colleague of mine, Sigrun Juliusdottir, a distinguished professor of social work at the University of Iceland, tells the story of a fifty-year-old man whom she remembers from her earliest days as a child protection worker. He'd grown up in an orphanage and suffered great hunger while those who minded him, round with triple chins, kept a storehouse of food safely locked in a kitchen pantry. Fortunately, among the many chores the boy was expected to do for the meagre rations he received was helping out the town blacksmith. His wages, of course, went back to the orphanage.

"One day, while the blacksmith was making a second key for the pantry, he left the shop long enough for the boy to trace a copy on paper. Later, using wood, the boy carved himself a key that he used to sneak into the pantry at night, stealing only as much as he needed to satisfy his hunger, always careful to leave no evidence of his secret. He wanted, of course, to help the other children, but he knew that would surely result in his getting caught.

"Years later, Sigrun met the boy when she was locked out of her office and in need of a locksmith. The man who came to her rescue was none other than that same hungry child.

Things Our Children Need

A child's resilience is always a reflection of the world in which the child grows up, not a quality of the individual child alone.

"There is a thin line between the problem child and the child who thrives. It is not just a child's spirit that decides his life course. It is the child's caregivers and the world we conspire to create around a child that determines which child grows up to have problems and which does not. If this sounds too simple, that's because it is. Or can be. The problem is knowing how to provide children with what they need in ways that are meaningful to them."

I stand up and reach for a marker, then write carefully on the flip chart a sentence I've already put on cue cards. I ask Ricky to pass one to each parent.

I'm hoping they'll remember what I've just written long after the group ends.

Merlinda inspires me to believe they will. "If I'm understanding what you just wrote," she says, "you mean that our children need us to make the world around them a great place to grow up. I think you said it the first time we met: change the environment and the child changes. Just like we've been doing with Sadie."

"And Jemell," adds Tina.

"Amanda, too," says Katherine, completing the round.

"And yet we still persist with the gross, victim-blaming belief that if only you are smart enough, fast enough, lucky enough, and enough people like you, anything is possible. I just don't buy it. Try telling that to the AIDS orphans I've met in South Africa and Tanzania or to street children in Thailand and Colombia. It's the same closer to home here in North America. Our children's individual characteristics are important when it comes to surviving during tough times, but those traits are not as important as what we, as their parents, teachers, and elders, provide them."

"Change what we do, and our children will likely change?" Katherine repeats slowly what I've just said, wanting to be sure she understands.

"You've got it. A child's motivation is only a small part of what prevents her from having problems. It works like this," I explain, sketching numbers and arrows on the flip chart as I speak. "Take one hundred kids and raise them in a crumbling neighbourhood where the jobless rate is more than 50 percent, most of the homes are occupied by single parent–led families, and gunfire is a common bedtime lullaby. Some children will survive that mess. Most studies suggest that perhaps 20 percent will emerge unscathed. Another 40 percent might not tumble into delinquency, but they won't manage to do much except recreate the same cycle of poverty their parents experienced. Forty percent will develop serious problems requiring vast sums of money from the state in terms of prisons, hospitals, addictions counsellors, and mental health facilities.

"But there are simple solutions — and everyday heroes making them happen. Like Victoria Durrant, who runs Angel's Nest in Whitehorse, an after-school drop-in centre and shelter for street youth. A mother on welfare herself, Vicki started the centre on her own, cajoling a local bar owner to loan her a storage building behind his downtown establishment. Cobbling together donations, Vicki grew her project to a service that meets the needs of hundreds of youth every day, providing a hot three-course meal each evening, computers, an arts studio, and a safe, quiet place to hang out or do homework.

"Cleverly, she has also found ways to link the kids to professional service providers by insisting the professionals cook before they counsel. Vicki assigns them to the kitchen for months before she lets them run workshops for the youth. It's not long, however, before kitchen banter turns into serious talk about the dangers the kids face. Everything from violence to drugs, sexually transmitted diseases, and school expulsions.

"'What the kids really want,' Vicki told me, 'is to connect with adults as real people. I'm like their mother.' She was right. If you looked closely, you could see Vicki had fashioned from charity a homey place that the kids could count on to be there for them. And in the centre of it all was Vicki, ever ready with a sympathetic hug."

"So, build it and they will come," says Tina.

"Exactly. Angel's Nest is a place where new stories start. Where kids get what they need."

If we had more time, I'd rant about the myth of the rugged individual and how we expect people to survive on their own, like the stories we tell about early pioneers and storybook heros. That's nothing more than a salve we put on our collective conscience to avoid the hard truth that a fair and just society — conveyed to a child through a fair, just, safe, and nurturing home — ensures that the most vulnerable get what they need, wherever they live. Suburbs or city, high-rise or detached house on a leafy lot. When we give children what they need, they are better able to resist becoming problem children.

When families can't do what they need to do, the world needs people like Vicki. What she does is not just good for the individual children she feeds — *it's good for all of us.* No more gated communities to keep criminals out. Safer streets. Fewer prisons. Communities that make the best use possible of everyone's special gifts.

"When I meet someone like Vicki, I think of a gardener. Plant a seed in fertile ground that is protected from pests and it grows despite itself. Plant it in a barren, despoiled patch of dirt and a few seeds will grow as much by chance as anything else. But for my money, I'd favour putting in a little more effort up front to guarantee I reap I larger crop.

"Even a seed lying dormant in sterile soil will germinate if given what it needs to grow. A tragic beginning doesn't predict a catastrophic ending. At least not if those who love their children do what they can to help."

With that, I go over to the corner of the room where I've left a covered plastic bin. In it are five bunches of potted daisies, all in full bloom, their white petals a traditional symbol of innocence and truth. They remind me of our children and the hope they inspire. One by one, I congratulate each parent for the effort they've made.

Katherine comes up shyly, takes her flowers, then gives me a huge hug. Tina and Ricky are next. Tina is happy to embrace. Ricky extends his hand, taking mine in one hand, then two, and shaking vigorously. Merlinda comes forward with Frank and accepts both flower pots on their behalf. "Thank you," she says and leans toward me to kiss me on the cheek.

Frank stands there for a moment looking at my outstretched hand. He pushes it aside and leans over me, his arms around me, his fist pounding gently on my back. For one awkward moment, we remain, leaning on each other, knowing there is much more that we need to say but won't.

Finally, as we all sit down again, I pass out one final cue card with a quote from Kahlil Gibran.

Though I began with an apology this evening, I'm realizing that more

Things Our Children Need

> You are the bows from which your children
> as living arrows are sent forth.
> — Kahlil Gibran

has gone right than wrong these past few months. If I have done anything well, it has been fulfilling my role as conscientious storyteller. I have woven tales to inspire these families to be their best. Where they choose to launch their children, however, is entirely of their own making. If they succeed, it is because they take the wisdom of others and fashion it into something that makes sense to them.

We've learned together that are no more problem children when parents help them flourish.

Chapter 16

A Last Visit Home

The group is finished. I still keep in touch with all three families, letting them know if things get bad again, they can always come in and meet as a family. Fortunately, none have needed to take me up on my offer. Of course, they have their moments of despair like everyone else, but their struggles are now a part of normal lives, their stressors are those of deaths and births and constant change. My own career has settled into a comfortable rhythm. I continue my research and writing. Most days, sitting in my quiet office, I'm deeply satisfied knowing I've resisted becoming another problem child.

I think I now know why somewhere, somehow, I found everything I needed, even if my father played only a small part in helping me succeed. Thinking about him this last year, I'm willing to acknowledge that he was a troubled man with too many problems to think about what others needed. I suppose he gave me as much as he could. A work ethic. Structure. Encouragement to stand up for myself. For a moment or two, even his love, though I've had to look hard to find it.

I still have no regrets for having not visited him in the hospital. He never called for me — not the first time he was headed to the operating table nor the last. I would have felt like an intruder. I'm not angry, just tearful, thinking about him dying a lonely man. Though if I'm honest, my tears aren't for him. They're for me and the worry I still have that my fate will be the same.

My mother is still alive, somewhere in a suburban concrete maze of shopping malls and overpasses. She hasn't seen her grandchildren in a decade. She hasn't seen me in more than seven years. Our last meeting was when I visited her and my father for a few minutes at their condo between flights on my way overseas. As heartless as it sounds, I have no need to see her again. My life is rooted where I am now, my past a stain that has been rinsed. To go backwards would bring nothing but new feelings of rejection.

I'm surprised, though, that I am pulled to see my father's grave just once. It's in a cemetery at the edge of a suburb far from anyone he would have known. Plots were cheap. On another Toronto stopover, while on my way to China, I rent a car and drive to the cemetery. The grave is just as my brother said it would be, on a small rise overlooking a valley with a tree planted at the graveside. Its roots are likely feeding on my father's wormy soil. Maybe this plot isn't so awful after all. It would seem he's finally found a way to anchor himself to a place where he can belong.

I reach into my bag and take out a half-dozen fresh bagels I bought on my way here. They are not Montreal bagels but they're warm, at least. I take a few bites of one, chewing slowly, then scatter the rest over the grave, sesame seeds dotting the soil like freckles. The bagels' calories are no longer a threat to him. Then I pull from my coat pocket a folded sheet of paper. On it is written *"Dear Dad, My apologies for writing you much too late ..."*

I crouch down and strike a match, pause, then reverently light a corner of the letter. It ignites and I leave it there on the ground among the bread crumbs as it turns to ash.

"That's for you," I mumble, then am surprised to realize I have one more thing to say. Something I've never said, nor realized needed saying.

"Thank you, Dad. For everything."

Nine Things All Children Need

1. **Structure**
2. **Consequences**
3. **Parent-child connections**
4. **Lots and lots of relationships**
5. **A powerful identity**
6. **A sense of control**
7. **A sense of belonging, spirituality, and life purpose**
8. **Rights and responsibilities**
9. **Safety and support**

I Still Love You © Michael Ungar, 2015

Things Our Children Need
1. Structure

- Children want a reasonable amount of structure. It convinces them that their parents love them.
- The structure parents provide children needs to make sense to the children themselves. It needs to fit with where children live, the dangers they experience, and the values that their families hold.
- Children are okay with being told no when what they want puts them in real danger.
- As often as possible, children need to hear yes and be encouraged to take responsibility for themselves and others.

I Still Love You © Michael Ungar, 2015

Things Our Children Need
2. Consequences

- Our children want the security of knowing there are reasonable consequences to their actions.
- Our children want to be shown how to fix their mistakes without using violence or bullying others that are weaker than they are.
- Our children need to be reminded they are part of their families, schools, and communities, and are accountable for the harm they cause others.
- Our children need quick and thoughtful discipline that models empathy, not harsh punishment that teaches them how to hurt others.

I Still Love You © Michael Ungar, 2015

Things Our Children Need
3. Parent-Child Connections

- Our children want to know that their problems are theirs to solve, and that parents are available to help them when they're needed.
- Our children really do want connections with their parents, but those connections will look very different at each age and stage of development.
- Our children appreciate the effort their parents make to connect with them. Parents need to remember what they've done right in the past and do more of the same in the future.

I Still Love You © Michael Ungar, 2015

Things Our Children Need
4. Lots and Lots of Relationships

- Our children live in interdependent worlds that bring them the possibility of lots of supportive relationships. Our job as parents is to help them nurture these connections.
- Our children need to feel they are needed and important. They need people in their lives who make them feel this way.
- Adults remain important to children throughout their childhood and adolescence.
- Our children need adults and peers who can help them build bridges back into their communities when their behaviour has made them outsiders.

I Still Love You © Michael Ungar, 2015

Things Our Children Need
5. A Powerful Identity

- As parents, we are mirrors for our children. We reflect back to them who they are and how much they are valued.
- Our children's identities are theirs to choose, as long as they don't do long-term harm to themselves or others.
- As parents, we can offer children substitute identities that are just as powerful as the troubling identities they may tumble into.

I Still Love You © Michael Ungar, 2015

Things Our Children Need
6. A Sense of Control

- Our children need opportunities to control their own lives and learn the consequences of their actions.
- Our children's experiences of control should match their age and ability. Children benefit little, if at all, from being burdened too young with decisions they shouldn't have to make and can't make well.
- If children abuse the control they have, the consequences they suffer should help teach them to act responsibly.
- Experiences of control give children an edge in life. They help protect children from being taken advantage of by others.
- It's good for children to attribute both their successes and failures to themselves when both are true.

I Still Love You © Michael Ungar, 2015

Things Our Children Need
7. A Sense of Belonging, Spirituality, and Life Purpose

- Our children need to know they belong in their families, as well as at their schools and in their communities.
- Our children need parents who will help them shape their values and beliefs.
- Our children need to believe their lives have a purpose and that their families need them.
- Our children need to know their culture in order to better understand who they are.

I Still Love You © Michael Ungar, 2015

Things Our Children Need
8. Rights and Responsibilities

- Our children need to experience their homes and schools as places where they are treated fairly.
- Our children need to be protected from racism, sexism, and other forms of intolerance.
- Our children need to be shown how they can talk back to people who exclude them or take away their rights. They need to be able to do this without becoming violent.
- Our children need to be given responsibilities at home where they are safe to make mistakes.
- Our children need to be valued for the skills and abilities they have and offered opportunities to use these for their benefit and the benefit of others.

I Still Love You © Michael Ungar, 2015

Things Our Children Need
9. Safety and Support

- Our children need access to the social determinants of health — things like housing, safe streets, well-resourced schools, and parents with the time to pay attention to them.
- Children, whether rich or poor, who experience physical and emotional neglect tend to grow up with problems. Give children what they need and they are more likely to be problem free and flourishing.
- Children who get their basic needs met, including opportunities to participate in recreational programs, are children who will feel better about themselves.
- Children who feel better about themselves are less likely to need expensive services like mental health clinics, social workers, and prisons.

I Still Love You © Michael Ungar, 2015

Things Our Children Need

A child's resilience is always a reflection of the world in which the child grows up, not a quality of the individual child alone.

I Still Love You © Michael Ungar, 2015

Things Our Children Need

You are the bows from which your children
as living arrows are sent forth.
— Kahlil Gibran

I Still Love You © Michael Ungar, 2015